BOOKS BY JOHN HOLLANDER

Poetry

Criticism

For Children

Powers of Thirteen

Powers of Thirteen

Poems by

John Hollander

Atheneum *New York* 1983

Portions of this sequence originally appeared in the following periodicals:

Acta Victoriana; *American Poetry Review*; *Antaeus*; *Bennington Review*; *Carolina Quarterly*; *Cumberland Poetry Review*; *Descant*; *Georgia Review*; *Grand Street*; *Harvard Magazine*; *Midstream*; *The Nation*; *Negative Capability*; *The Newark Review*; *The New Republic*; *The New York Review of Books*; *Pequod*; *Poet Lore*; *River Styx*; *Shenandoah*; *Stand*; *The Times Literary Supplement*. Section 19 appeared in *The New Yorker* under the title "A Moment in Maine"; sections 156–168 were published in *Poetry* under the title "Thirteens"; other sections were printed on broadsides by Iron Mountain Press and Palaemon Press. Permission to reprint all these is gratefully acknowledged.

For Natalie Charkow

Powers of Thirteen

This is neither the time nor the place for singing of
Great persons, wide places, noble things—high times, in short;
Of knights and of days' errands to the supermarket;
Of spectres, appearances and disappearances;
Of quests for the nature of the quest, let alone for
Where or when the quest would start. You are the wrong person
To ask me for a circus of incident, to play
Old out-of-tunes on a puffing new calliope,
Or to be the unamused client of history.
But tell me of the world your word has kept between us;
I do what I am told, and tell what is done to me,
Making but one promise safely hedged in the Poets'
Paradox: *I shall say "what was never said before."*

Refusing to Tell Tales

Late risers, we sleep through all the morning's heroics,
The triumphant winds of early light that blow the last
Rags of dark to pieces and sweep them away, the fierce
Levée of the flaring monarch of our globe. We give
All that high stuff the runaround, getting up in broad
Customary stretches of appearance, breakfasting
In the midst of things that have been going on awhile.
Thus we need not undergo the old delusion that
Comes from entering the day soon after all the great
Goings on, feeling that morning has been warmed by our
Work. Thus we need not add our own weariness to that
Of afternoon; and as far as endings are concerned,
One does not begin feasting at dawn, but at sundown.

None Too Soon

3

So we came at last to meet, after the lights were out,
At someone's house or other, in a room whose ceiling
Light was accidentally switched off—and there you were
In a corner where I had not seen you just before
When I had rushed in looking for someone else. Even
Then the shadow of an earlier time deepened the
Room—and this was before I learned that in my childhood
You lived across the alley-way, the light of your room
Crept through my window-blinds, throwing ladders of light up
My ceiling in the dark (when I was four I thought that
"Shadows" meant spills of illumination from without).
Then, years later, I stumbled upon you, standing next
To an unlit floor lamp, against a mute looking-glass.

The Shadow

4

At the various times of the year I have paid you
Plaintive visits, as on mornings when it was too hard
To believe that the fog would be burnt off before noon
By the very sun it hid; or moral ones at high
Midday, when hot shadows of how things seem are barely
There; or towards sundown when, walking up a reddened beach,
Cool shadows of long remembrance convening as one,
(Oh, that there were so much shade at the noon sun's great heat!)
I have headed your way at a recreative time.
But when we walk out at night, or early on some fine
Afternoon, all preliminary colloquies yield
Their various tones to the broad translations of light
And dark, laid on with late strokes, fit for our going forth.

Visiting Hours

5

At first you used to come to me when everything else
Seemed to have gone away somewhere—even those winter
Absences which themselves will desert cold orchards in
The January thaw, before returning the land
To its definitive hardness—and where a few broad
Strokes preserved the momentary pink, scratched at by bare
Trees, of winter twilight. Hedged around by denials
Of scene, we could deem ourselves to be the place we made.
Now, speaking figures of light, we redeem the barren
Plenitudes of picture, even in postcards and views
Crammed with the illustrative, as of the dumb head of
El Capitan at the specious twilight's first gleaming,
Or of lonely Neuschwanstein on its tinhorn summit.

Then and Now

6

Your bright younger sister whom so many fancy to
Be you was always getting in the way when your friends
Were about. An "altogether inconvenient child
With an alarming memory" one of them said once.
She would help you sometimes when a trick was to be played,
A pompous visitor to be derided, something
Lost, or broken, to be covered for; but for the most
Part, she was up to all her own mischief. From her touch
Nothing was safe. But then, what she did was all for show,
Nothing was changed, ongoings of every day outgrew
Her goings-on. But it is your doings that have made
The difference to me; I walk down the boulevard
With you unnoticed: her red hat makes everyone stare.

Fancy-Pants

7

Earth, water, air and fire were not elementary
Enough, after all, for our minds' desire—even though
They covered matter's three phases of solidity,
Flow and spirit, and commingled with them the hot light
Of thought and passion interfused, and made up four good
Candidates for the noble order of foremost things.
But then we multiplied the simplicities, until
The periodic table folded up. Now again
The elements are four: I myself, whose hand and heart
And inner eye are one and indivisible; ink,
Discursive, drying into characters; the hard, white
Ground of this very page; and, for the fourth, yourself: air
In which I burn? Or the fire by which I am consumed?

The Elements

8

Lying in love and feigning far worse (we love to know
That show of pain consumed it and none was left to feel)
For so long we had made up dozens of excuses
—Excuses for making up excuses they were—out
Of the stuff of love. Ah, but even saying it makes
The heart sink: what do we make things out of—need? desire
To have, to make? Or rather out of whole cloth? Or yet
The tattier fabric of vision and oversight,
Undersong humming along with it all, Gretchen's wheel
Spinning its own disco music? This can go on and
On, but what of candor now, of truth? We must reflect
On this obscurity with a bright, open face, not
Foolish, and musingly look at the dark and light up.

The Pretext

6

One evening in early spring Father gave us dimes:
George planted his in the hard and sour ground of the yard,
Hannah pasted hers to a card and drew crayoned wings
About it, little Willie lent his to a playground
Friend who never paid him back, and I—I took the dime
And let it lie among other coins in my pocket,
Hearing it jingle, safely hidden away among
The ringing gathering of its own kind, like itself
All unspent and all quite blind to just what being saved
Had meant—loss of glitter in the places of exchange,
Of all the energies of getting and expense. Yet
It could sing out: my dime could rhyme with its own echoes,
Down inside a buried sound it was no death to hide.

Hidden Rhymes

The power of "might" that makes us write—the possible
Worlds without you in them that takes so much describing—
Reveals the poverty of what we can never have,
All those echoes, in the dense, thoughtful forests, which can
Never speak their own minds, all those images which would
Have flashed across the faces of our amenable
Mirrors, had the world been otherwise, the want of you
Been part of its unwisdom, as it were. As it is,
Naming you for what you are, taking you at your word,
I have pushed my way through the thickets to the treasure
Of onlyness, of the immense wealth of our one world,
Yet wary of its edge, as where our selves cast, in this
Hidden wood, unkind, black shadows of unlikelihood.

Feigning and Necessity

May-day, the day of might, day of possibility
That became the name of cries reaching out for help from
General disaster: it has come and gone again
With all its shows of power—the phallic mayhem round
The village pole; the parading of the red banners;
The branches' payday after weeks of budding, silver
And gold of first blossom yet unspent in the heyday
Of later flowering. Then June will waste her substance
In riotous living, then that auxiliary
Verbiage with which the sociable seasons discourse
Of their own vainglory will parade itself and raise
Ruckus enough for millions of dancing villages,
Scarlet petals enough for all the new worlds in earth.

Aftermath

Dahl and Forsyth, Freese and Fuchs, Weigel, Wister and Zinn
Stand about my piece of the land, making it their own,
Chatting along the fence, standing tall at the corner
Of the lot, or clambering up a white column on
The porch to have a look-see into the neighbor's yard.
In a noise of color, spring empties itself into
Summer, rumoring of more, better and worse, to come,
Flowers laughing in the sunlight of their sprightly names.
Earth will write them up in its book of rising accounts
Even as the names of my locals get written out
In their discoveries, their illegitimate get:
Spring-weekend-and-summer people, some regulars, some
Nonce visitors, seem to be taking over the place.

Summer People

13

In search of a note I half-remember your having
Written me, I went rummaging through the table-drawer
Over by the window. Half-stuck at first, it opened
At a jammed angle and all I could make out inside
Lay in a scattered jumble: blunt, small scissors some child
Had once been given, a matchbook from the old Chambord,
A half-crushed shuttlecock, three dulled pennies, a crescent
Inchlong moon from a jigsaw puzzle with cutout shapes
Hidden in it (part of a mirror in the picture).
The tales of their entrances into the drawer are not
Your story or mine; but what they were doing for years
In the dark, preparing their piece of astonishment,
Is just the matter of our quiet conspiracies.

Half-Opened

14

I am preparing a perpetual calendar
Out of what might have been mere journals (a page a day,
False confidences, commonplaces commented on,
Perhaps a pressed wildflower here and there, all of which
I find will not do for you) and some half-printed leaves
Torn from copies of the Farmer's Almanac in years
When it had been quite wrong about the winter's weather.
(Counting the days till, say, next August the whatever
Has never been your way, who have always made them count.)
There is a season for every time, and thus I rule
Boxes and fill them with new songs and ongoing jokes,
Not the matter of what merely happens written down
But written up, in this old ledger, the true account.

Never Out of Date

The shad and asparagus are over, the berries
And late bluefish still to come: and yet beyond these wait
The successive New Years at harvest, mid-darkness and
Arisen spring—three points each of which could be a pure
Spot of origin, or a clear moment of closure.
As it is, they whirl by as bits of what is being
Measured rather than as milestones, as parentheses
Which turn out to have been what was being put between
Brackets in the first place. Occasions usurp the false
Fronts of giddy centers on circumferences. How
The lazy susan of the seasons turns around! piled
Chock-a-block with delectables, eased about by Time,
Our most thoughtful and, ultimately, murderous host.

Beginnings

I stood under a plain tree discoursing with someone
Lovely and young, or lay out upon the fancy lawn
Remembering a faraway body, recalling
A lost and distant laugh, recollecting disparate
Instants of delight in other seasons, other lands.
I stared down the halted water under willows that
Lay shadowed upon the dark shallows, and held my oar
Like a breath, the faraway wail of vanishing cars
Hanging in the active, evening air, my heart empty
Of souvenirs, my mind unwinding its arguments.
All these are within your nearby memory: remind
Me now of some moments mirrored in oblivion
As we stand silent beside some silent summer stream.

Amenable Locations

17

What there is to hear from the particular sea-mews
Homing in on our local point cuts through clarities
Of fair evening and the difficult radiance
Fog exhibits, high-noted observations whose tone—
High, personably middle or far from simply low—
Is muted by the sheer pitch of the wingèd outcry.
What there is to see in the running out and back in
Of our local inlet sighs, through barriers of firs
Along the low intervening islands, with rumors of
The ocean's legerdemain, which by mere sleight of land
Keeps taking back what ground it appeared to have given.
What there is to know from the touch of the silent wind's
Hand gathers these raw reports and sifts them for the truth.

Clarities of the Coast

18

The low wind, the loud gulls and the bare, egregious cry
Of a goat somewhere around the point the land urges
On the unteachable bay: these have taken of late
To commenting on our two forms—differently placed,
Each observable only in quite another kind
Of light—posed silently, sombre-hearted among them.
What they say is as unfathomable as what we
See, gazing out between mildly distant islands at
A horizon contrived by gray sky and gray water.
The nearby green water, with no memory of all
That distant amplitude of sea, slaps playfully at
These contemplative rocks which might be ourselves but for
Our darkening power to behold them and compare.

Further Clarities

The pine with but one thought regards the water against
Which it rises, the wide bay with so much on its mind—
Clumps of nearby island and smudges of distant rock,
Other firs at the end of the long meadow which cut
Into the water's extent of consciousness, and at
The faraway edge of the day, an elaborate
Serial narrative of sundown. Now a long yawl
Crawls wearily into sight: the pine of one idea
Points to it as if it should remind the water of
Something; but the bay, as if in some old joke about
Absorption, is reminded of the sky—everything
Reminding water of the sky—despite its bazaar
Of reflections. This puzzles the single-minded pine.

Opacities of the Pine

Firecrackers sounding like shots of handguns rattle
The afternoon of early July at a late time
For celebrations and it is an inglorious
Fourth we have come to, like the birthday of a very
Sick man: no simple affirmations will do today.
In the dying wind the nation's stars and stripes slacken;
I guess this must be the flag of its disposition
Not to save itself. Only now, much later, all flags
Down for the night, we watch some bunting—no more a flag
Than the flag is our old glory—as it fitfully
Gleams in the streetlamp's conditional light, like a truth
Which the sad, difficult telling of half-conceals, half-
Discloses, through our few tears ungleaming in the dark.

A Late Fourth

21

Oh,
    say can you see
    how our old
    ten and two and
        one
Our thirteen starters twinkling, an original star
Flared up, a July fourth supernova, (memory
Watching starry rockets now in grandstands, or along
Chilly beaches) Can you see how then it exploded
Westward, southward, urging the hegemony of light
On hills of high, darkened cloud, unwilling plains, milky
Rivers and one-candled mountain-cabins of the night?
Democracy which closes the past against us (said
Tocqueville) opens the future up: but as you sit here
With me on the high rocks at Cape Eleutheria,
Truthful in your shawl, all the light that ever was shines
In your eyes, later to burn off tomorrow's blankness.

22   *Sparklers*

I have burned batches of cookies, formed rich tortes all wrong
From the start, propounded all-too-consistent puddings,
Lost hot cross buns, fussed unduly over cupcakes, turned
Bread—in one of those mundane, negative miracles—
Into stones, caused popovers to burst with windiness,
Launched Zechariah's flying rolls, filled Ezekiel's
Edible one (lamentation and mourning and woe
In equal parts, rising eloquently in long pans).
Now I am at the work of confection even when
Loafing, not irrelevantly, near the oven door
Where what goes on is no longer in my hands. All these
Maker's dozens come out right: I read your recipes
Now, remember your arm firm around the mixing bowl.

Baker's Lament

13

23

To say that the show of truth goes on in our outdoor
Theatre-in-the-round may be no more than to remark
That one is always led out of some cave or other
Into the irritating glare of what is never
More than a high, wide, sunny, open local chamber
Of our general system of caves. But that it plays,
Night after night, under lights, drawing crowds even when
It is most archly stylized, let alone when lines are
Mouthed, and crotches scratched, in flatly stylized masquerades,
Means more. Truth sank all she had into this spectacle;
What's behind the scenes is openly part of the show,
As is everything that you lean over and whisper
To me knowingly as we watch one of the tryouts.

Long Run

24

When to say something of what stretches out there toward me
—Greens, rock grays, colors of water making up spaces
That speak to what we dream up as distance and depth—seems
Uncalled for, one is almost made to reproach oneself,
Asking, *How can one sing a strange song in the Lord's land?*
Mouth evasive and emphatic scat-lyrics of all
The mess of exile, there at the heart of a place famed
As the terminus of the longest expedition?
And yet, what had made one abandon each land was the
Blaring of some general canto, whose unisons
Comprised their own imperious mode of noisiness.
One rejoiced in an inward air as one underwent
Wandering: here still one must intone that undersong.

By the Waters

25

The universal great space, stately but ungrounded
Never seems, on star-guarded nights of enormous width,
To be our proper room, wherein we are, but rather
Where we are ever on the brink of being immersed
In what is beyond us and our being in the know.
And yet, on clouded midnights, all that outer black goes
Utterly blank, all the grains of light dissolving in
A mist of the implicit and the occluded; we
Are welcomed into what is a dim, high-ceilinged hall
We might as well be lords of. Impossibilities
Of too much openness having now clearly closed down,
The waters above muddied as if somehow for our
Own good, space retreats and makes way for us, and for room.

Our Place

26

I try to go new places with you, and yet we keep
Returning to so many of the old ones, sometimes
By lazy design, most often inevitably,
Given the unmapped ways that we take. This afternoon,
For instance, far up the beach people were gathered round
What would have had to be the event of the season:
A clam playing a harmonica or something like
That; and our walk along the wet sand where foamy hands
Kept rewriting their marginalia was halted
Short of that novelty. We were left with the renewed
Singularity of sundown behind the sand dunes,
The commentary that an eastern sea out of which
The sun rises keeps making upon the book of hope.

New Wrinkles

27

Words we have exchanged keep playing out their low treasons
Against the journals of the usual, the nocturnes
Of the odd, falling into line once they are uttered.
The parts of our discourse, which stretches out of sight far
Ahead and long behind, wait with the patience of those
Who have been truly used. Or far less complacently,
Twenty-eight thousand, five hundred sixty syllables
Here breathe hotly down the neck of some ultimate one
That may not demean their manyness. Means to some end,
They have been awaiting death. Endings mean meaning's end.
So the final monosyllable, with a volume
Thunderous and inaudible brings us to a close.
In the end as in the beginning will be the word.

At the End of the Line

28

I went out without you yesterday for a slow hour.
The lichens which in the right light give a choral tongue
To the rising rock were simply plastered over it;
The fir-woods began just at its circle of shadow;
The sun leaked down to the floor in interesting ways;
Here was here and there was there; all sorts of life astir
In among other, larger things were there merely for
The noticing—and yet noticing was not itself
A kind of drawing of breath, murmuring of pulse,
Let alone the mind's caress which shapes and loves at once.
Everything was clear and one thing: nothing came between
Me and where I was, there, amid a manageable
Jumble of evidence. This was this. And that was that.

The Fact of the Matter

What she and I had between us once, America
And its hope had; and just as I grieve alternately
For what I know myself to have lost of what had been,
And for all that loss I was suffering all that while
I was doing, I thought, so well, so goes the nation,
Grieving for her hope, either lost, or from the very
Start, a lost cause. All our states and I are one in this.
O my America, my long-lost land lady of
The hardening ground, the house neither ancient nor in
Good repair, the brackish stream, the half-abandoned mill,
The red plastic bucket that hung in the place we kept
By the beach where, I remember, August evenings
Rang with hilarity until we trembled with cold.

An Old Song

With you away on whatever other business you
May have, or going for a swim (the day being hot)
In perhaps some forest pool, all I can do, I find,
Is question or provoke. I wonder among the deep
Shades of my dusty study with its single candle
While my wandering eye surveys, in wild fields beyond,
The rusting iron in the ripening corn; I hear
What the July hot air noises emptily about.
Without you around to take seriously, I ask
"Well?" of the wind; "What?" of my dim working-place; "Wherefor?"
Of the rustic emblems of latter America.
The sad, ungainly cows of our land look up and mourn,
"Who needs a gadfly on the way to the slaughterhouse?"

Summer Questions

We are all at sixes and sevens not just about
The state of the nation but our state of contention
Itself, you maintaining that repose is a snaffle
In exuberance's mouth, I that quarreling is
A cave where the spirit sits deafened and dumbfounded.
You rise to the bait of what I refuse to stand for.

Arguments of heat cool off in bed where arguments
Of light are dimmed in horizontal ways of being
At odds. Rough, pleasurable strife resolves nothing but
Minimizes differences for the while we lie
Silent together in apposition that is true
Friendship. —*No*, you say, as if to awaken sleeping
Amity to its daily work of debate once more.

Nay, calls strife's reveille. I disagree; and we're at
A new kinds of odds, in which my braying out of *Yea*
Shivers the morning air into little blasts of wind.
But this smacks far less than ever of domestic farce—
No fear lest dinner burn, say, while unheated, genial
Discourse propounds itself in the next room; no fear lest
Argument drop idly to the floor like a dishrag
The while Judy throws what was to have been lunch at Punch.

Your side of the story? Starting out with unhoarse nay—
Saying? Well, without me, you would never have it told:
Your tacit dissents are heard only in inference
From my affirmatives, yeas echoing unheard nays.
I'll give you eight to five that at bottom we agree.

Disagreements

After one of our unheated arguments, I heard
Two shepherds (well, not shepherds really, but let us say
They were) contending, beneath a verdant shade about
To give in to autumn, over their contention. A:
All of what we say in the first cool of early fall
Can only be a palinode to parting summer,
A recantation of easy heat. Sez you, says B,
What we sing is a prelude to the sober beauties
And late passions of the ember months. Says A, *To be*
Truthful for the moment——interrupted B: *For Aye . . .*
But both agreed on you: how in your very breathing
Their debate resolved, in the A, B of your heartbeat.
(I can assure you of this, who made these shepherds up.)

Eclogue

Wholly concerned for the mass of the pieces that we
Carve day by day, we feel none the less put upon when
The consequences of their profiles are finally
Laid at our door. But how not to have what we had meant
Remain forever on the under-surfaces? How
To keep what it had been all about from lighting out
Suddenly, the night before completion, with what cash
And negotiable securities there were? Keeping
The finished piece in darkness is out of the question;
Yet not minding that it will be got wrong is harder
Than carving itself, than the work of roughing-out fine
Attention which, not like an abused servant giving
Notice, rather trembles on the verge of taking it.

I thought that you might have something to recommend in
Re this plague of misunderstandings which come buzzing
In when we run up the flag—on some holiday, or
Perhaps to show the children how it is properly
Done—and hang around in a brown, noisy cloud until
Hours after sunset. You have seen such visitations
Come and go, and I picture you smiling placidly
Through the most alarming crowding of the summer nights
With the stings and wails of nasty, pick-up orchestras,
Or, attended by the two young Misses Construction
And Apprehension, presiding over an ornate
Interior. Proof, yourself, against being got wrong,
You I hope can show me how to cope with all of this.

Being Got Wrong

Well, now, the year having finally come to a head
Here at the end of summer, you and I can begin
Again in the crispness of things: the new honeyed taste
Of a bright, hard apple of the early fall, the look
Of the next chapter in the annals of yearning as
Reflected in the quickening of its bright first page.
But the brightest leaf turns over, its shadowed face down
On the dark ground. We thrust into the middle of things
Even at their start, surprised by the forenoon's fine snap,
By the skip half-hidden in each of our steps, thankful
To have been preserved and sustained by the very wind
That blows away the summer, to have reached this season.
We will have to look into the matter of winter.

Very well, then, what now? There are resolutions far
Easier kept than made, acts of connection between
The speaker and the spoken-to (and -for) easier
Done than said: you know this well, whose speaking is my deed,
As I, remembering a quiet listener of
My youth, whom my inept, yearning touch penetrated
In a smooth moment and darkly dazzling, for which
There were no words and never would be. For the new year
I shall not promise you anything more, then, than what
Is strongly done even if lamely said: "I'll try";
"I will be tried"—hard threats hidden in soft predictions.
You, who promise nothing, thus ever give, as you have,
With your eyes, the gentle smiling of impure surprise.

Starting Up in the Fall

38

Where has it gone, that long recent summer when the mind
Sported with waves along an ever-brightening beach?
There was a long look to be taken both up and down
The miles of strand toward where dune and sky vanished in light.
Wisdom had come from the wizening of Christendom,
It seemed; gleaming chariots would leap forth on the land
At the sound of the breaking of all the cruel old chains.
Around the bonfires at evening, ceremonials
Sent up sparks into the black air: the drawing aside
Of the curtains of flesh revealed what in the firelight
Appeared to be the figure of joy, yet bondage lurked
Invisibly in the shadows of the emptiness.
Summer gone, what work is it we must get back to now?

Cool Days

39

The fall wind, a maddened Santayana, rips the leaves
Out of the volume of our lives when the day's reading
In the chilled park is over; a sibyl of rubble,
Who flings them no great distance to where the garbled heap
Of verbiage goes on with its old unsightliness;
A discounted cantor who intones the text about
Which we shall always be outraged and against which our
Bookish bodies yet cry out like leaves composting in
Their hay for our now unrestricted clay, when the last
Worms shall have their treat and dust shall be the serpent's meat;
But at the last, a word-swallower at the great, red
Autumnal fair, who silences our last dying moan
And snuffs out the final rhymes of breathing with his own.

Destroyer

We ramble along up-hill through the woods, following
No path but knowing our direction generally,
And letting fall what may we come up against the worn
Fact that all this green is second growth—reaches of wall
Knee-high keep appearing among low moments of leaf;
Clearings, lit aslant, are strewn across old foundations.
This is of course New England now and even the brook,
Whose amplified whisper off on the right is as firm
A guide as any assured blue line on a roadmap,
Can never run clear of certain stones, those older forms
Of ascription of meaning to its murmuring, as
We hear it hum *O, I may come and I may go, but . . .*
Half-ruined in the white noise of its splashing water.

One of Our Walks

If I were a different person with a different sort
Of occupation, I might show you, on some late walk
Through a part of the city you had not seen before,
My place of business; you might even meet a few of
The workers there, their presences graced by anecdote
Perhaps, and then we might stand out on the pier looking
Over the harbor and its lights. But I own no mills
Of dark red brick; so walk no further than where we are
Now: meet my unembodied helpers—Jenny, spinning
Out the thread of discourse; Dolly, trundling along her
Bulky objects; Jack lifting and Doc Crane unloading;
Poor lazy John who cleans out the gleaming bowl; and bright
Molly, bolting the tall gilded mirror to the wall.

Where I Work

Now I walk with you through the ruins of the city
Of Glyph, low piles of rubble on a low hill under
A baking sun, shuddering at how close to nothing
A wise king's walls and postern gates became. Like all true
Ruminators over wreckage we console ourselves
That words may still strike live sparks from even this dead rock,
That enchanted documents outlast the monuments,
Marmoreal dust survived by the memorial
Light of the word. So with me conversing you forget
All time, and amid the ruins of ancient chaos
I stand with—and I want to say, "thee"—making a fresh
Start, in an oasis of our saying, knowing that
We will be outlived by what of green we have given.

Ah, but the lions of time sharpen their claws against
These rocks of book, wearing away powerful reasons
And sovereign rhyme; and the old tale they told themselves
—The moony-eyed idolaters of broken columns—
Was that their scrawls would endure, even as the endeared
Squares of the sidewalk where they played marbles in the spring
Outgloried Rome etcetera. And if the whole tale
Does not exactly crumble into mindless dust, still
All words lose their sizzling edges in time, blunted
By inexactitude, our race being unable
Now to heft any weight of meaning. So with our words:
Your heart hardens; my will softens to wool; your sight sighs,
And my wide mind narrows its grasp to what is merely mine.

Some Walks with You

24

This whole business of outliving—it is as if, once,
One mild summer evening we were sitting outside,
Eating a few leftovers, when two great Presences
Came by, tired, and in their gentle way quite ravenous,
And we shared all of what little we had with them, and
Not that the bottle and the few bowls refilled themselves,
But that you and I were emptied of our appetites
That mild summer evening under the slumbering
Green of low trees, and that the departing Presences
Left us with the gift of a common moment of death.
An old story. Yet for all practical purposes,
When I go, you go—whether or not a laurel bush
And a myrtle just then spring up there outside our house.

But for all impractical purposes, you'll outlast
Me, who'll endure not in memory, merely in soft
Clay. You were around before we met (I, too, but with
That fascinating difference we keep trying to
Figure out): whatever you taught me was for your own
Survival, even though I've subsisted on it too.
Talking you up as I do among unlistening
Branches and heedless gardens, beside uncaring parked
Cars along a noisy street, may just be playing down
Your words, as if the script of summer midnight you were
Starring in were one you couldn't ever have written.
What will it be, then: a condition of evergreen?
A state of starlight? We'll consider it for a while.

Talking You Up

How charming—magical, fragile both, I mean—the time
When Past was like a dungeon, Present a wide forecourt
Looking further out at open, sunny future fields;
Or when some hidden room in the dark house of childhood
Had to be ransacked to profit what one hoped to be.
Not so now: the Hall of Records is all skylight glass,
And the starlight of the coming centuries which winks
And beckons will have been coming from aeons before.
Yet, loosed from the dark past, looking out through the picture
Window of California at a mile-wide future
Unformed save at the hands of the moment's comfiness,
X sips the honey of unproblematic sundown
And takes a long drink of the milk of amnesia.
Y, back east, asks what came before us, and what lies there.

Letting in Light

The figure ahead of us on the trail, looking back
From an easy stance of pause belying the extreme
Difficulty of the country: he has gone before
Both in that it was in the past that he trod the ground
Which now we stand on looking at him with far less ease
Than he, and that he waits before our gaze like a part
Of the high trail itself. His glance, open but clearly
Asymmetric, borrows flashes of sunlight among
Leaves of underbrush to do its winking with, winking
Of acknowledgment that he knows what we know of him,
Preposterous graybeard with a touch of the farouche,
Behind us and ahead of us at once, one eyebrow
High overarched there in his momentary bower.

Still, the trail lies all before us. Neither alone, nor
With a tour, you and I walk our own kind of *via*
Media. Even when he or she accompanies
My rambles of the afternoon, you will be walking
At my other hand, pointing out how immediate
Presences—the gray, unquestionable rock I see,
The untranslatable, loud wind I hear—yield themselves
To the scentedness, warm of blood, full of heart, of the
Living thing midway between them. Moving up the path
With you is as if mounting some trim companionway
From the ingenious turbines up to the high points
Of lookout, not rejecting where we had been before
But bearing a part of what was into what will be.

On the Trail

An anecdote: I sat here in this chair last month, and—
Wow! you came up right behind me, startling me so that
I broke the last word off the line I had been working
At, abandoning the feature-story of despair
I had been fashioning, and turned back to see whether
You had deliberately crept up to rob me of
The last word, or whether simply to tell me someone
From Porlock or from Washington had telephoned me.
What ever could you have thought to do with that missing
Word? Pelt me with it, as with a berry in a broad
Field of fruited bushes we were slowly moving through?
Feed it to me, in the starlight, in some ultimate
Rebuke? I'll never know, but you've helped me mend my ways.

The Last Word

Your games of hiding: the one you played this afternoon
In the Memorial Park, where you walked by the lake
(The shadow upon it of the old bow bridge was more
Of a way of getting across reflective water
Than the cast-iron arch itself): one moment, and you
Were gone. Then I heard laughing from the rocks that I used
To play on as a child, mica winking in the sun,
And saw you standing half-hidden in a niche, shadows
Of frivolous leaves falling across your summer dress.
Your other game of hiding in the dark ... In return
I play my games and bury an old coin in your cake,
Or put an artificial pressed flower between two
Leaves of my intimate journal where I know you'll look.

And Go Seek

Now: There was a tall girl once whom I mistook for you
—Or was it you I thought was she? (Just like a tall tale
From some lovely book that I had not allowed myself
To see the figurative meaning of at all). My
Heart was dim, the lady's name was light; how gently once
We sang, I now remember, in Indiana in
The summer night, and she warmed my distant winter that
December. Unchained to the letter now, your spirit
Plays hide-and-seek, now in the fair and tall, now in the
Dark and small. I am most near it sometimes when hiding
My impatient eyes, counting to fourteen, piercing your
Disguise. Here I Come, Ready Or Not. Where are you, Love?
The tall girl's long gone, it is a summer night again.

August Recall

All the singing rivers commend our rivery songs:
The estuary at New London hummed an old theme
Softly in the revised standard version of the Thames;
The harsh Jordan, narrow enough in the Middle-East
In the middle-west snaked through the campus, a toy stream;
The slow Charles led me to its source in the trickling Cam.
The East River wedded to the river that is west;
The conjunctive Harlem, where to spite the devil once
I spun in a folding kayak with an older guide;
The dirty Cuyahoga; the tall Connecticut;
Tiber and Danube, Rhine and Seine of which enough said—
Who will chant the silence that celebrates their orgy
Of confluence when at last they join the Stygian flood?

Principal Rivers

53

Patterns of light and flakes of dark breaking all across
The surface of the stream—rhyming words of wave, strophes
Of undulation, echoings of what just had been
Going on upstream a ways—we like to take all these
As matters of surface only, as part of the shaping
Or framing of the banks. But that would make the water
Stagnant and silent, whose face gives no interesting
Access to its depth. Yet when the brook gets to babbling,
Really has something to say for itself, the surface
—Broken, flashing, loud—changes place with what depths there are.
Then what forms on top will have been troped up from below,
And the otherwise soundless and motiveless bottom
Will be constantly noisy with the figures of light.

Reading the Brook

54

Mademoiselle de la Moon gazes at her gleaming
In the ever-hungering sea's midnight waves. "My Queen,"
Sir Water seems to sing, "I am subject to your light,
Your will betides well or ill for my very motions."
Yet the wailing main need not crave favors: he has made
The cold moon up, projected her out of his flashings
And phosphorescences onto the fire-bearing night,
Rolled his wet lamplight into a round mirroring rock.
His rough surface shapes an object to be subject to.
There are too many reflections on mirrors by far
As it is for me to dwell upon the parable,
And for once the firstness of the sun does not apply:
This is a matter only of moon and ocean-light.

Reflections of Desire

That great, domed chamber, celebrated for its full choir
Of echoes: high among its shadowed vaults they cower
Until called out. What do echoes do when they reply?
Lie, lie, lie about what we cried out, about their own
Helplessness in the face of silence. What do they do
To the clear call that they make reverberate? *Berate,
Berate* it for its faults, its frangible syllables.
But in this dear cave we have discovered on our walks
Even a broken call resounds in all, and wild tales
We tell into the darkness return trimmed into truth.
Our talk goes untaunted: these are the haunts of our hearts,
Where I cry out your name. Hearing and overhearing
My own voice, startled, appalled, instructed, I rejoice.

Under the Dome

We need not visit this big metal archway in which
The not-too-distant other shore is framed. In the west,
A famous bold parabola propounds its puzzle.
Here, far from that high paradigm of openness, looms
Our local hyperbola, more thick and squat, merely
Huge. The writers come to gawk at its blandly smoother
Curvature, to misconstrue its inner space, which is
Only an emptiness, not a leaping-up of room.
Admiring its high gleam, they do not see the mocking
Dark lower branch of their hyperbolic arch extend
Itself downward, dropping through the complementary
Air above some park at the other end of the earth,
The statuary of admiration doubly botched.

Travel Note

The Queen of the Parade floats by on her painted car,
Glitteringly, in between postures—sitting for some
Endless series of portraits? lying for the moment?
Standing for the brave Muse of Parading who could not
Make it this afternoon? Ten streets ahead The Old Men's
Band plays *A Closer Walk with Thee* as chromatic tints
Of something bouncy in another key fall across
Its dying sounds. Held down by long guy-ropes in the hands
Of struggling lackeys, the Great Forms float by overhead—
Pegasus, Apollo, a Hippogriff, Daffy Duck:
In childhood, knowing that these balloons were full of air
Deflated in no way whatever stature they had.
Now we gaze sadly, bored, at the Triumph of Moments.

But the Queen will not be forsworn. She turns her head, smiles,
And waves at us amid even more oompahs, sirens
Cutting the distant air, seducing all attention
To the violent island all around us, away
From this tacky-tawdry ill-timed progress, this parade
Of tired fables which is now an institution.
But the sirens are tired too and have all belonged
For some years to the Society of Sound Effects.
They are as part of a neighboring parade the Queen
Will also loll amidst, begrimed as beglittered now.
Her smiles go on for miles; the great balloons will preside
Over the darkening streets, over the lackeying
Layers of lower air they gravely bow and sway among.

Pageant of the Cold

The Fun-House of the fairgrounds once stood here. Inside were
Contrivances so tacky that, far from scorning them,
Now, we value them as antiquarian machines.
No restoration could bring back the effects—the room
Of multiplications; the mazes inside mazes;
Reversing chambers where we were condemned to getting
On with things ass-backwards. Jokes—about penetrations,
About the One and the Many, about buggery,
Were born there, buried now in graffiti (*One can buy*
Balm for any disappointment:/I'll board you forward
Without need of ointment—as if that could end something!)
When the doors slid shut behind one and there was dark, that
Was origination; when they opened into bright
Sunlight, that was closure. One was out of there for good.

Public Landmarks I

The old Melpomene Theatre right across the street
From the Gaiety, itself a singer of sad songs,
Was in its time a revival house and now awaits
A new developer, someone who will see that when
Its old façade is broadened slightly, its back wall brought up
A bit, the shortening of the room will yield no less
Depth, and more flexibility for the inner space:
Ad hoc arrangements, temporary rooms, openings
And closures, so that one will be more free in less space.
This house of ex-*aiaiai*, scene of the formerly
Tragic, this theatre of recapitulations
Then will shed new light in an old place, whatever may
Be playing there, ancient words watching from the shadows.

Public Landmarks II

It was not for such fragments that we wandered so far
A field, a mountain, an old city by a river.
But more and more the broken pieces we saw in our
Meanderings came to have a power to command
Devotion that the unfractured images themselves
—Venus entire, a solemn family on a grave
Stele—could never have had at their time, let alone
From us. So we see these interruptions of an arm's
Extent, these abstract structures replacing familiar
Dispositions of the body's tribe of parts, these shapes
Of breakage passing over faces like traces of
Thought, and knowing how they figure our way of being
In our bodies, we believe in them as in ourselves.

We consider this archaic maiden who has lost
Her head over time, and gained her patch of fractured stone
Here, along a newly conceived plane, more personal
Than the half-ineffability of her fixed grin.
Stone can hardly be in pain, yet this has undergone
Something beyond its original shaping, something
Beyond that origin of feeling an inner edge
Of the outside world, the end of oneself. But in the
Light of our dry brooding, figure yields its truth to form;
Form returns to marble; and to broken stone we cry
"Good! You deserved it! What flesh has always had to know
You now have learned." Yes, but when stone has been turned into
A trope, what we see fractured here will be heartbreaking.

Breakage

63

Here by the ruins of this fountain where water played
With stone while the light was playing with it, long sessions
Were held on pleasant afternoons, with talk of shadows
Seated on the sunny grass, of substance there along
The marble benches. There they walked together with their friends
Laurie, Stella, Delia, Celia, Bea and the others.
But over on the hill there were those who spoiled the fun—
Dirty old Dick Dongworth, his mighty line no longer
Standing for him (when their stichs go limp even Uncle
Walt's dildo won't do for them any more), and Louise
Labia, her heart an open book—eye your body
From their past, as we pass by the places where they lurked
Jealous of the others, too early to have met you.

Dreams and Jokes

64

Now that you bid me write of what she and she-sub-one
And she-sub-n and I did at those various times
Of darkness in the working day and the knowing night,
My truant pen writes with French letters: *je, ma muse, et . . .*
Your laughter hides in the spaces of my stammering.
We may be our own blank sheets, but ink can never come
Clean about the heart of matters like those you remind
Me of, our oldest sports played on the fields of ourselves,
Our briskly-danced adagios that now enact the old
Moments from behind their zigzag comitragic masks.
But what are the words in amor's low language for deeds?
All said and done, Love's wordless sword is mighty as the
Pen is, which mars our sad amusing talk of Venus.

Your Command

65

Heroic Love danced on our stage awhile, in the dark
Of the days that shone and shook with Heroic Battle.
But that act was over by the time Sir John Failstiff mocked
Love: "Sock it to me—that's what half-mooning's all about,"
He chortled, brandishing a dirty sock. Even then
The slack-jawed face appealed to the bumpkin in the hay
Or in the back seat of the car, its wordless message
Flashed out "Have me, I'm hopeless" or blinked its "Now now now."
Now the dance is Love for All, love well lost for the world,
The risks taken are those of intimacy; love fell
A casualty of the unceremonial,
Laughed at by the wind in our heckling, red leaves, themselves
Gone the way of the whirled, fallen to mere easiness.

The Lovers

66

In the old anecdotes of amor they still allude
To in brittleness of feeling, the master of arch
Ceremonies, the perpetrator of injustice,
Takes after his father Mars who, they keep forgetting,
Is always in the picture; and thus they can complain—
Speaking of earlier enactments of their cases—
"On love's disputed ground, on bed of war, they both lay,
Fallen soldier, fallen whore—how unfair, this falling!"
As for falling in love: O, if one were said to rise
In it then—all being foul in these matters—so should
One have to rise in battle, or asleep, as if one
Thereby were moving away from—rather than toward—the,
After all, irrelevant fall of our finale.

The Fall

The crime of Onan probably was not that lonely
Joy, but sullenly refusing to get on with his
Brother's business, choosing to cop out suddenly, there
On the spot. This was the lonely sorrow he begot:
Abandoning the work for dream or musing, not love
Of hand (in neither case abusing self, or delight
Or some poor Other's lot.) But if just now, I withdraw
From some well-loved form that lies here, half-done, half-composed
On the lined sheet where we have come together, it is
Hardly to shun the work of making, but to get on
With it, turning, in the darkness of our lamplit tasks,
To your new phantom, lying by the old one you fled,
But with me ever, body in body, hand in hand.

The Abandoned Task

68

All our cheap, failed love-stories are old tales told even
In the dear language of Paradise: Poor Al F. finds
That one hot, urgent night on the front porch comes to mean
Not just having Beth, but ever after having her
On his hands (she is no mere doll it turns out). A roll
In the unmown hay keeps unrolling an alphabet
Of episodes, the tête-à-tête descends to fumbling,
Then the consequences of the cough of fulfillment.
Lamed Memsahib of noon, she limps through the tawdry bush
Of daily life. Who is to pay? The frail-bosomed fay
Lady of the car back-seat and queen of the front porch?
The fancy dancer who barked his shin on the next day?
Their sin was surviving their desire. The end was tough.

Literal Account

Like some ill-fated butterfly, the literalists
Try to pin down—its illustrious wings extended
Not in eloquence, but unwittingly—the fragile
Spirit of doting, at all those layers of remove
From brass tacks. Yet after all, brass tacks get lost in time,
While what one was asked to get down to them from endures.
Thus: young, before sweets of doting had soured into doubt,
I made an idol of the image of her figure,
Until one soft night I found it squirming there beneath
My grateful but unbelieving body, in a bed
Borrowed but smooth with moonlight—at which the idol was
Destroyed, its shaping of desire usurped by the skill
Of remembrance, in her realm of frail-winged images.

Lepidoptery

Like prisoners released from cells built by their touching
Itself, hot walls firming up every hot new minute,
Bars worming gently into place with no more clanging
Than the close sound of breath, one after another they,
The lovers, emerge into the quiet after-court.
The sobbing of their bodies . . . for loss of what had gripped
Them, as for joy at being outside themselves once more
Their soft jails, spun out of their hearts . . . I would not have said
"Cocoons," but you pointed to the window-glass, battered
By gypsy moths, imprisoned without, souls in ancient
Mysteries, alighted on the corners of windy
Pyramids, fed on the wisdom from lacy pages
Of the now-tattered hieratic book of the woods.

Soul and Body

"*Pleasures and pains, pleasures and pains, when a man's married*
His songs are refrains, his texts well-worn misquotations,
His passionate homilies unwittingly cribbed from
The standard handbooks of harangue."—This itself, quoted
From some other well-meaning manual, is as one
With the "passionate homilies" it would interpret
In just the way the homilies did not want to be
Taken. What can we learn about Wisdom, then, from all
The Handbooks of Handbooks? What avails the way in which
Cool, old voices of distance are heard screaming? in which
Homely points of needles and pins bright and dulled, grander
Views of homeliness, and yet loftier points from which
Grandeur is put in its place, stand on the same cold ground?

The Foundation

Oh, yes, the animals were a hard act to follow:
Through all the stages of creation, the vaudeville
Of coupling unfolded until without much of an
Intermission the first of us were sent out, partners
Evolving their routine even on the night itself.
Thus that now old business of human-see, human-do.
Had we come on first, rather than late to our last act,
Had beasts learned from us to come together in benign,
Obedient turns, what of our nobler parts? What of
The wing-caped, glittering rider of the fierce horses
We are now below the waist?—High and low, anima
And animal, all one in us, bodies entering
One another would be our most figurative dance.

Animal Acts

The aftermath of epiphany was not just yet
Once more a round of delights and celebrations of
The vision of misrule; no delayed instant replay
Of the party; no mere lowering of last night's jests,
Sir Toby Fart now on a diet, Malfolio
Grousing in some incomprehensible dialect.
The Low was always there, wedded to the High before:
Rapt Viola fiddled with words, diddling them till they
Came; the copulars of syntax played sexual parts
Of speech in the oldest learned jokes. Our afternight,
A bit longer, sadder, even more contrariwise,
Has turned the banquet tables on the wearied games that
Put decorum, poor devil, in his own hell of fun.

High and Low

When, aping the literary lover, his eye filled
With one star, I at eighteen tried rhyming into bed
A tall, dark girl named Barbara, now dead, everyone
Had an earful of my earnest conceits, studious
Wit, and half-concealments of the way I'd hoped we'd end
Up; and the more contrived my rhyming became, the more
It meant about desire (this the ear-filled ones could not
Understand). I marvelled, dazed, at what was done by less
Textual souls for fun; I hoped to, like the girl-shy
Yeats, pass through the tenderest of gates, and discharge with
A mighty spasm in her deep, romantic chasm.
The truth was that, though she and I rhymed a few times, my
Young words on their paper sheet had far more joy than we.

And thus in writing "of" this one or that, sending open
Allusive letters to A or elusive letters
To the world in re B, I was arising from the
Dreaming cot of language onto the teeming streets where
A's and B's and ampersands awash with C's and D's
Filled the air with their din. We had not met, nor could I
Have heard your soft voice if we had. All this is just to
Say yesterday I found a second-or-third-hand
Copy of my earliest verses, Barbara and
Willow-willow and that ilk, inscribed—of course—with your
Name. After a while, some moving-day, you'd passed me on.
But it seems that some fair monitor even then made
Lust and wit hold hands, heard passion in the studied leaves.

Erotic Lyrics

When we were all fourteen, the sharper our visions were
—Say, of the body of the neighbor's girl at her bath
Framed in the half-opened window across the courtyard,
Say, of her memory of young Heathcliff on the black
And white screen that afternoon—the more distant from touch.
Staying in a sense fourteen, even as we were all
Getting older, kept something alive—the girl's image
Blurred as she lay beside us in the bed of springtime,
The actor's face coarsened into color and substance,
Yet the Sublime kept climbing its ladder as the flood
Waters rose from the cellars; something beyond contact
Kept touch constantly aspiring to it, even when
The mind wandered, even to being fourteen again.

The structures and agitations of the older ways
Of handling matters of love, then housed and empowered
Other spirits—it was as if an old tomb could be
Recast and made into a series of monuments
Of reconsideration, with the base as of old,
A new frieze, somewhere in which the antiquarians
Might discern an image of the old tomb as it was,
And a new roof open to the stars. But these places
Are empty now: neither lovers, nor thinkers in the
Light of the afternoon, lurk about them any more.
But they stood for so much more than they were built to bear,
And for so long, memorials to the masonry
Of the ideal, as if love hung ever aloft.

The age of sixteen, in its infinite wisdom, puts
Lightly aside mere fourteen's joys and terrors. And thus
With our larger histories: the temples all rebuilt,
Modern love went it all the better, hung two more strings
On the old, echoing instrument, strung two more lines
Across the alley-way to hang the dirty laundry
Out, for the truthful wind to comment on in detail
(Underpants flapping like the triumphant flags of love
Smocks blown into the clefted folds they had been worn to
Conceal). Now, when love and thought take their evening walks
They linger to talk along the widened peristyle
And slightly lowered elevation of a folly
Like this one in the public gardens we know so well.

Songs & Sonnets

Let's call it quits: I never long for you any more.
But the matter of your voice low in the late lamplight
My heart minded over for so long, the substance of
Your morning shadow dancing on the floor as you dressed,
The evening shadow of your body's depth, stand here
Demanding some ceremony now. Some fuss. Let's call
It quits. Addressing what I've just said, you reply then
Cheerily, "Hi, Quits!" We giggle and have done for now
With lying, not against half-truths so much, but telling
Tales against the other—falsehood—halves of whatever
We really mean by saying what we feel. "Hi, Quits!" "*Quits*"
(Like all his clan of feelings) grumbles, not at the joke,
But rather at having been given a name at all.

The Resolution

A book: as I read it the letters keep decaying
Into illegibility, as if they had been
Poorly xeroxed to begin with. I awake, seeing
Behind my lids the blank of erasure and hearing
Only the surrounding murmur of four walls, hummed in
By silence, and asking if this meant you would leave me.
Even as I write this dream down my pen consumes it,
As the page's famished surface uses up the pen.
That the pain of most private loss could not be published;
That without you I remain not nothing, but something
Blank; that the dream-book's roughened leaves turn to green again
Only because you allow your paintbrush to be used—
These darken into truth as in sympathetic ink.

The Dream of the Book

Once you and I—but no fables now. Tell what there was:
Once within a place she and I were together in
The way that fictions about our lives can be: each one
Feeling not for, but by means of the other, so that
Soft converse in the dying daylight penetrated
Both of us, who therewith felt each other's and our own
Deeps; and acts of darkness in the quickening night made
Discursive the room, the house, where all were imbedded.
But after, away here in the noise of circumstance
I scribble alone at the old story: *Once upon*
A time, she and I were together in the way that
Only those who have had the intelligence of love
And the experience of loss can etcetera.

"Yes, go on! This is plain talk of plainer feelings now,
Passion and pain in their imperative moods," cry the
Ninnies of experience. Fools of the omphalic
And the literal nod in comprehension. The soft
Coins stamped "STRONGLY FELT" clatter down the receptive slots
Of the automata of actuality, who
Start in on their dance of being deeply moved. When those
Unstrung puppets wind up their timely and mindless act,
All the ninnies buzz off to supper. Then you and I
Are finally alone, beyond the din of their ken.
Moonlight enters our unlit room and projects a bright
Shape on the wall outlined by our shadows, a figure
Of our connectedness, of what we have between us.

Twice-Told Tale

Meet me here in the middle of the woods where I am
Making a path out from the clearing that you showed me
Months ago (now so overgrown with a thick muchness,
Merely more of the same—nothing summing it all up).
Moments of maximum penetration leave one with
Minimal resources for escape, and the thread of
Memory is all I have to lead me out of this
Mess of amazing amusements I've been working through:
Mid-forest musics (Haydn in the woods?), overnight
Mushroomings of weird, pale incident. Come find me now
—Mind the turning ways!—and we'll make do: there's more than wild
Material enough to stretch. We are two, but there's
Making what you always lovingly call both ends meet.

Letter

The heart of the matter? It throbs laboriously
—X says—amid shovelfulls of exasperation,
Neatly sawn cords of tedium, and sorting out brads
From endless nails. Not so—says Z—it leaps trembling at
The first strains of the body's serenade, at the light
In the clear blue window hinting that the door below
Will soon be unlocked. But at the living core—asks Y—
Slightly off the center, does not the pointed, rounded
Emblem cut into the contemplative tree not lie?
What Y means in the matter of the heart pictured there
Is that such inscriptions to the long moments of pause
On our walks beat out a general pulse: you and I
Figured in cut letters, the point of it all, the source.

The precisely central point of anything must be
Another matter, though. Small wondering schoolboys will
Submit a compass-pinprick, or an *I*'s dot that might
Mark out a dead center, to a microscope and see
The point getting lost in a wide, vague range of middle
Ground. But in its most contracted state the center stands
(Everything lies around it, it is about nothing),
Center of origin, equidistance, silent rest
And pointlessness. For only in the meddling schoolboys'
Destructions of certainty do areas arise,
Dim, jagged of bound, unexplored, in which one might roam
Ever dangerously, yet safe in the dark knowledge
That mapping these places means covering everything.

In the dim, indeterminate part of these woods, where
What we broadly call the middle of the excursion
—A place of being most amidst, not at an exact
Point of center—one has been ascending all morning,
Pushing on with joyful effort. Here is no-man's-land,
Ever contested for by starting and finishing.
From here on, downhill all the way: children run and laugh,
The older ones begin to creep, struggling now against
Descending itself, more than in the worst up-hill climb.
It is worse to have gravity pulling one onward
Than tugging one back from behind, restraining mere wild
Leaps upward. After the middle that grim force drags us
Not back to a starting-point, but on to the last place.

The Midst of It

87

These two tales I tell of myself and the life I led
To its destruction, one dark, one bright: one gathered from
A few gleaming moments—a slice or two of the cake
From where it was perfectly marbled—the other one
Rising from an undersong of despair. In neither
Case is the truth of the story—or the story of
The possibility that either one could be true
Or false at all—of any interest. What matters
Is what they might be good for: the story of a lost
Joy, as a sad anchor to drop below the surface
Of where we keep on going; the other version of
What was, the tale of a hell escaped, easily sounds
Like a noisy breath of wind filling my patched old sails.

Tales of the Sea

88

I'd not thought that drowning would be so like an easy
Ascent of some low but quite important hill: the tank
Into which I was descending of my own accord,
Lined with the light of some pale blank green, I was surprised
But not disturbed to find was set with convenient
Hand-holds for speeding one's progress downward with. But then,
As if you had recalled me in my own voice somehow,
Or as if some deeper shadow in the tank had stayed
My sinking, I turned quickly from shallow sleep, sank back
Into the self whose image I was when in the tank.
Telling you this now, I learn that the drowning-dream meant
Nothing, but would merely (had I not let go the hand-
Holds and turned up toward my bed again) have been my death.

The Dream of the Deep

The lion is the king of the beasts. We are the ace,
Contemplating his tawniness, color of dusty
Sunlight fallen on stone worn smooth; contemplating yet
The crown that his very image in itself upholds;
And, finding in his eminence the type of our own,
Seeing it was our high eye for hierarchy that
Enthroned him. Even now we know that others exceed
His power—the cow who shod and fed the white hunter,
Mannlicher in his bearing, the trypanosome in
His blood that brings the lion down—these are fierce satraps,
Victims themselves nonetheless, of the lordship of man
And of inhuman disaster. Two careless jacks thus
Dispense the bidding of the one-eyed great lord of life.

But now we are talking of what lies beyond the range
Of the visible, away from the gaze of the old
Hand-held cameras, beyond the ken of old John Reel,
Gnarled, reasoned white hunter of desire, huddled over
The spoor of the moment, which can lead him only on
Into the uninterestingness of the high grass.
The king of being hides in the labyrinth of size,
Not of mere turns of the way: we must move inside the
Very traces of traces themselves—there must we go,
Within, within, to find his double-spiralled cord spun,
Once thought, by the fates, a gossamer thread that leashes
The lion and binds our destinies, poor jokers, who
Still take our few tricks with the lion's magnificence.

Our Dominion

Cutting pages in a book—upward, across, again
Upward—I hear the various leaves sigh in their own
Several tongues: *"Enfin!"* whispers the slim, gray volume
Evenings in Marrakech (I translate); *"Endlich!"*—this
From the serious, sick treatise on "Unendingness"
(As close as English can come to that); and a long gasp,
"At last!" from the great folio of my earlier years.
Facing pages must at least once in their lives get to
Look out even at a pair of idly focussed eyes,
Let alone up past them to some kind of ceiling; light
Must be let in between them, lest the blind marriage of
Page one forty-four to one forty-five imprison
Them in their locked, unembracing gaze, their bundled sleep.

Chopping down a tree with names carved in its bark, mine and
Hers—not unwittingly, like some frenzied or condemned
Hero of high romance initiating our brute,
Obstinate compulsion to outlast our good names for
A while, but like a homesteader of the great heartland
Clearing a space for what will come to be—I took less
Of an ax to the past than the present already
Had, and heard no desiccated Dryad cry out *"Ouch!"*
Or *"Remember me!"*—the tree was no poetical
Oak, but softwood, waiting to be pulped, rolled, dried and bleached.
And it is you I now stand eye to eye with above
This ruled page that mirrors each to the other, while yet
Hiding my face from my own gaze, yours even from yours.

Opening Up

51

"Every soul is unique, and, thereby, original:
It is only when it employs the body to make
Something of something else, or utter something, that it
Falls into the nature of being imitative."
—So Doctor Reinkopf, overseer of the leaky jars
Of our lives. If he is right, the uncracked pots we shape,
Our noble tombs and numberless innovations, all
Come out of old Being-in-the-Body's pattern-book.
What of our walking, then? One would not want to remark
"What an original way of walking *that* is" if
The lurching or creeping person so indicated
Were crippled or lunatic or winning some dumb bet.
What of *our* walks? yours and mine? All from old Baedekers?

Well, Reinkopf?—*"I suppose that every soul, exiting*
From its crackpot body does an original dance ..."
We dare say that he'd say so. But we two must work out
This matter of ambling, this walking out into things
We have been doing. *Walk* holds *talk* and *work* by their hands,
Between—yet beyond—them both, perplexing the Doctor.
The body's stride and trudge aside, our strolling involves
Our soles and our wingtips equally beating against
The pavements of the pure air and the clouded sidewalks;
Whether gliding through the rainy town on errands of
Light, or idling in some brightened mews at midnight, or
Making the city's great *paseo* late on a fine
Afternoon as shadows beckon to the lights of shops.

Body and Soul

All flesh is as the glass that shatters, through which we see
Within, and cannot do without. Thus as we both gaze
Through this wide pane at the morning haze the ground exhales,
Distant, shrouded mountains and these younger, nearer ones,
Shoulders bared and nudging elbows with each other, all
Seem to paste themselves against another kind of plate,
A pane of air placed between where they are and the glare
That presses its face against this picturing window.
The reflective window meanwhile is half-mirroring
The mind of someone—you? me? or are we of one mind?
—Someone glassy-eyed and starry-minded who surveys
These giant ridges and furrows of thought lit up with
Points of high color where cars crawl along hidden roads.

All glass is as the flesh which refracts its energies
Because of something unseen within it, which is framed
So that the seer and the seen are both beyond it.
Glass through which we look thus reflects our very looking;
So bare limbs embedded in mountain landscape conform
To each other's curving in the body's second thoughts.
Some buried eye of touch peers through the transparency
Of thigh on thigh, hand shaped to breast; this gentle fiction
Lasts a moment only, though: in the next light body
Mirrors body, flesh touches other flesh, by feeling
In touch with itself, as in fables that the clear eye
Whispers to what it can see through, toward what it is out
Of touch with, candid old tales of distance, space and glass.

Behold!

97

No sun shone for so long during that long summer that
Candles everywhere in the land burned with a gray flame.
Gold had become dull, and lead like tar, and the demesne
Of sunny meadows shivered under a foreign reign;
Master craftsmen downed their tools halfway through every piece
Of work, not for enjoyments, but to start on the next
Slightly inferior one; the standard musical
Pitch wandered through a major second from town to town,
And as for numbers, weights and measures—But then you came,
Surveyed the hopeless scene, and, yawning, closed the Big Book
In which all this had been written, shelved it heavily,
And wrote a laughing letter to the whole afternoon
Of great enterprise and beauty (yesterday, this was).

The Old Tale

98

These labor days, when shirking hardly looks like working
Yet sounds far too much like it . . . standing idle, I muse
On which of us two helpmeets, when we weave together,
Is the worker, which, unwittingly, the noisy drone.
Warp might contend with weft for priority, wrecking
The whole frame, wrenching the time into a travesty
Of a day of rest. Were the hum of our shuttling song
Stilled for long, the thin lines strung across the workaday
Loom would sag or snap. But back-and-forth breeds up-and-down:
The figures develop in the field, growing under
The sole working light of our attentiveness. Where would
I be without you? Who ever see you save through me?
United we stand and shake the chains heard round the world.

Back to Town

Once we have grown to a certain size, the very means
By which life is kept in trim come to be those of death;
And for anything larger than a village meeting,
The instruments of the eternal vigilance which
We know must be paid out for liberty are themselves
Chains. So that liberty herself is tithed after all—
A scrap of her drapery, a lock of hair, one more
Wrinkle each minute, filling despair's hope-chest so that
Our freedom may still breathe. How long can this go on? Like
All beautiful creatures must this one too then consume
Herself? Such questions scatter in the light autumnal
Winds, and the point of asking lies buried like a pin,
Hidden, that yet stabs you and cannot be turned away.

The way the hills of Umbria look so movingly
Like their painted versions—a way not of rhyming nor
Translating, let alone of mirroring—had to grow
Up in order to behave like this. Had long ago
To put aside childish things of looking back across
The wide valley through the stony window into the
Widened eye and narrowing gaze of the painter there,
Or of leaping with joy at the sight of its image
—The image of its own mode of resembling—taking
Over from the image of hills, which same had just been
Edging out gold leaf as the stuff out of which backgrounds
Were made. Had to come to where it is, and we are, now:
Our ways our sole high deeds, our roads our destinations.

When our sense of nobility could yet be measured
By a glimpse of a wise Duke appearing plainly at
A window-seat above the courtyard of his handsome
Palace, it was unthinkable that some day the whole
Thing must needs invert—the Duke with his famous profile
Then would sit upon the pot, and the only emblem
Of what in all of us he had once represented
Remained obscure, lurking somewhere in the crowd's catcalls,
In the health just of debunking, the Bronx cheer, the flung
Dung, the mocking jeer with which we hid our sad fear of
Praise, the whipping away of all the old scenery
That was the only act of worshipping left by then.

And then the lusty scorn of noon became the idol
Of the next day. The Scoffer, all sincerity, cast
Hugely in bronze by means of the usual lost wax,
Was raised to that sad eminence in the Plaza, where
The statue to avoid before had been the one of
The local hero, General Whatsisface. *Mocking
Having hardened up into piety, what shall do
The joyful heroic jobs now? What shall represent
Our true Altitude, nobility smuggled within
Its guise? Surely not the old Horseman restored, surely
Not a figure lit by engines of bedazzlement*
—So they wondered, so asked in the privacy of their
Committees, wondering whether to report at all.

What of the Plain Man then, who walked about unadorned
And unadored? He had his brief day, his time of few
Words: "Here's to plain dealing and plain speaking" said the fat
Man; "Mr. Seward, may I have a pen; I'd like to
Do some writing," said the tall one on the train. O, their
Famous fables were pasted up for a goodly while
(Not born aloft by dutiful lictors, nor peering
Through blue greens of waving gonfalons). Those were the days . . .
But what has plain speaking come to? Not a foppishness
Of its own frivolous simplicity—that, one could
Bear—but the long look slowly dropping to the bottom
Line; the flat terrain full of echoes whimpering in
The face of one's dying; complaint as explanation.

There is more to plainness now than the unwrinkled brow
Can reflect. First of all, the work on Simplicity
Being done at the lab out in Evermore has led
To the cracking of the plain; but then, too, the immense
Difficulties in the way of making what was plain
Easy to grasp—the lack of handles that are affixed
Any more firmly than with stickum to the surface,
Any reticulation anchored in something deep—
Made researchers give up the traditional approach.
The plain may be a wild mine of fancy, dancing nymphs
Of trope turning about in (not even below) its
Broadest reaches; flatness full of the creatures of our
Connections; assonance in the silent-growing grass.

—Or it may not: either way, the sense that we can get
Away with skating across the old pond that always
Has been frozen over at our time of year is now
Beset with worries. And the question whether to post
Warnings or not becomes moot when no one around can
Read signs to the littlest of children. Experience
Writes its fables, you may say, in invisible ink,
So that the story-lines of our day-to-day romance
Are unaware of their relation to the text of
The exceptional upon which they comment without
Wisdom, but with some technical skill. If only we
Were simply less than noble! There would be no problem.
General Whatsisface on Horseback would seem sublime.

The thin journalism of our attachments: even
They who write the stuff are seldom caught reading it now.
And it is only when something cannot be given
Away, that the sidewalk vendors start doing just that.
That what the morning brings, then, comes in baker's dozens
Should prove no surprise. It is a little bit extra
That stands for there being a whole lot less than there was:
The gray wheelbarrow full of green and gray ten-dollar
Bills, falling lightly and leafily along the way
To market; the length slowly accruing to shadow
Late in the day when the clock has already been set
Back an hour; what will have been consumed by the time
Harvest has rolled round again, with its great, reddened moon.

Speaking Plainly

107

For years now we have been getting so used to shoddy
Work, that when something finally comes along that has
Been carefully formed—with pains taken that surfaces
No one will ever see have been finished, and the best
Stuffs used in the old, unimproved-upon ways—we can
Only distrust the whole contraption. Ways of phrasing
Stone, metal, glass, fabric, wood or words that are lazy
About the times, careless of cheap ways we do things now,
Are an overworking of seriousness, labored
Doings in a spontaneous bed. Something too well
Put elicits the sense that something is being put
Over on one. So, lying here, guitar untuned, I
Loosely strum according to the wind, and am believed.

Taking It Easy

108

When to raise a voice in song was to lay down the law,
Repetitions—even of what once had been commands—
Fell like caresses on us; and those with the dumb ears,
For whom the chant could only drone, danced about the strange
Metal images and spun in the newfangled whirls.
At this the songs grew querulous and once more and yet
Once more corrected the defectors, then fell into
The unyielding ostinato of the paving-stones
Pounded into place, the thudding of sameness, the next
Buttonhole-stitch, the next spot-weld, the next turn of the
Wrench, the labors of love that should rather be its works.
Had not song gone its own wondrous, its own lawless way,
Imperatives would fall on us in joy and beauty.

New Dispensations

Watch the potter as he botches his product, throwing
The piece, that should have been a monument to beauty
Lately banished from symmetry, with a sick motion
Of the wheel, a disturbed caress of the hand, yielding
A tired, ill-shapen lump that falls apart from itself:
So do we mis-shape our lives, inept at Providence.
Watch the welder as he wields the hot allying light,
Sprung from the marriage of foul air and pure, scarring the
Line of the join with the assertive seal of joining
Itself, a rabid priest who weds simple villagers,
Demanding that they take his name: so do we marry
Our seasons, days and years, the flailing blades of our will,
To the great, shaking I-beam. All clatter in the wind.

Watch the besotted glass-blower hiccoughing into
His growing bubble of dream, ay me! the moment of
Involuntary withdrawal of breath, spirit chopped,
Lasts in a brief, bright eternity of crunch preserved,
Of clear globe gone to blast until he crushes the whole
Glassy disaster beneath his heel, and it cuts him:
So do our inspirations fail, all our personal
Crystal worlds smash into gossamer and clear eggshells
At our stuttering of breath, gulpings of our desire;
So do all the consequences of what we do fall
Into some version of the adversary again.
Watch the weak weaver—he knots his yarn into nubbins
Of nastiness: so do we coarsen our every veil.

Watch the carpenter teach an old saw to sing again,
Ripping away along the grain of his pine plank; his
Back-and-forth, his in-and-out of the cleft of the wood,
Lower his blade toward the silences of motionless
Sawdust. Unwisdom's buzz-saw sends us scurrying back
To the self-righteousness of handiwork, the hoarse sound
Of the coughing apothegm that can hold true because
It never meant too much: so do we move back and forth
Again and again, renewing nothing, coming to
The end of the distinction we had drawn in pencil,
To the end of the period we had been sentenced
To serve, to the implication inherent in our
Sawings: the old meaning to which we had been condemned.

Arts and Crafts

In former times all apprenticeship was in itself
Triumphant: the hand of the master lay half-hidden
By, half-glowing through, the nimble enterprise of the
Studio. But that system has long since disappeared.
Indolence, impatience, the whole tax picture, make it
Impossible to get or keep assistants. With each
Man his own master *"Instant Mastery, Now"* is sprayed
Everywhere from cheap paint-cans. So I and my splendid
Apprentices have a secret agreement: Hugh Wood
And Carrie Waters—their very execution is
So brilliant that no one looks beyond that—keep their wise
Peace and silence, content to learn that the better they
Get, the more there is to know; content to outlive me.

Shortage of Help

How can one expect monuments to be preserved when
Even our legally protected dreams crumble to
The dust of half-remembrance? Or all the scale-models
Of places we had loved or feared—O, in a meadow,
Her straw-colored hair interwoven with green, where once
We took cool umbrage at the sun's clearest light, and found
This place, singing with our own desire, yet eternal,
As if topaz-colored rivers flowed out from the land
Around us, as if all other beds and fields would be
Pictures of where we were now, and the embroideries
Of flowering branch worked on our sunny bodies there
Were prefaces to many shadowy verities.
Memory had preserved that private park fairly well.

But when, in want of being in some kind of touch with
Tremblings and glories of an older sort, I intrude
Upon a spot like this in vision, pushing branches
Noisily apart to see her body still embraced
By the green ground, it falls to ruin: there is nothing
But the laughter of the pressed-down grass where she, lying
With her silent and adoring tongue, had lain with me
On a young June afternoon when my breath and hers were
A piece of the general wind. Today, my hearing
Rings with the silent palatal that can make *now* know
Something of *then*: my eyes melt in truth come in sad aid
Of late time: my memory shivers as dark footsteps,
Somewhere, disperse pretty posies laid across her grave.

A Landmark

Arachne spies by the door on wise Penelope
To learn what will be her own undoing. By lamplight
She sees the busy shuttle going back on itself
With a more fabulous skill than when, that afternoon,
It had been proudly building the fabric of a shroud.
Taking apart the cover of darkness fabricates
Light, and Time itself goes forward by unravelling:
So the queen's dismembering hand weaves the images
Of faith and remembrance on the bared warp of her loom.
Arachne ignores the lessons of nay-saying that
Lurk in what she sees there in the midnight's unworking.
Her eyes are only for the energies of resolve,
Of what is spun out of oneself in devout silence.

Such emblems of old craftiness that are clear enough
Still to read, point to the one step forward, two-and-a-
Half steps back that everyone eventually gets
Used to. Now you sit on that red prayer-rug, undoing
A dark scarf, skeining the wool in puzzlement, as if
The process should not be still continuing, nature
Having forgotten when to stop, knowing it too well.
But we need not despair of negations: bits of yarn
Snipped far too short for knitting were tied, knot after knot,
Onto the warp and weft of some Anatolian
Frame, shunning all human figures for the intricate
Shapes, "purely decorative," geometric, that lie
Refigured now with shadows of your hands in firelight.

Fancy-Work

64

Which of these pictures of you shall I keep? An early
Portrait from life? Perhaps the famous scenes, paintings
Done from other pictures for which, in a sense, you "sat"
Far more directly than anyone but I could know.
Or perhaps the old painter's favorite, the somber
Shadowed portrait that he fancied best "either because
He himself was conscious of having failed in it, or
Because others thought he had" (although we would feel more
Comfortable if our own favorite had been his).
I must choose one of them, I who never learned to draw:
What my hand could not manage to project in a plane,
What I can't develop on flat canvas, I shall have
To talk about, to remain a bulky chatterbox.

The Likeness

The wildly-colored girl with her round belly twisted
Further around, as one might twist a plum on its stem
In plucking, her face whacked apart into its aspects,
Steadies the pier-glass full of her reordered image,
Truth having made a mess of false beauty against a
Battlefield of screaming lozenges, all the carnage
Of decoration. Across the gallery the same
Painter allows another, linear, girl to go
Unviolated, guarded by the god of his sad
Heart, a fierce metamorphic beast who caresses her,
Thus warding off the violence that his shining, dark
Eyes would have otherwise commanded an obedient
Brush to execute, as on the girl across the room.

Between these battle-scenes in the wars of figure and
Form, she sits on a low bench and holds up the round glass
In the lid of her compact to her unviolent
Regard. Her tan hand emerges from the gathering
Of the clans of like tone—buff and beige and wheat and bran—
On the plain of what she wears. Beside her, with his hand
Extended to her tan knee as if to steady it,
He has eyes only for hers, she, for the monocled
Gaze of her mirror; yet in these sundry objects each
Espies the object of desire, but invisibly
Disguised as an image of itself. Those two will tear
In time their images, wreck the very subject of
Desire more wildly than whatever the painter wields.

In the Gallery

66

You must have been peeking at the sketchbook I carried
About last July: it is open to a sheet of
Hopelessly ill-tempered crossings-out; I couldn't catch
Flying scraps of darkness swallowing the summer light.
On the facing page I had had a quick, mute go at
A tranquil pool of bay in the late afternoon fog,
Silence that had to be broken to be remarked on.
You must have seen, too, why I had to give up trying
To draw: the pure syntax with which the great, creating
World is written whispered to me to take up this pen,
Leaving the Faber pencils to someone else, for whom
All those spaces between the letters would silently
Present themselves as figures of deeper lettering.

Thus my refusal to walk beside you with even
A camera nudging my ribs: some pictures taken
Along on our rambles—still lifes, or interiors—
Are aids to reflection, like shades or binoculars.
But taking pictures of wherever we go can serve
Only the spirit of recollection, mother of
Outlines and keeper of the précis. Memorials
Of what we have seen are better made of murmuring
—Ours, and the voluble world's—, by leaving every
Question unanswered, but nobly responded to with
Later questions, whisperings about what was whispered,
Low melodies hummed as the words to the overheard
Tunes of what there is, giving its account of itself.

Travelling Light

Here is an old album of wood-engravings—not yours,
But perhaps your sister's—and something neat has been done
To them by way of collage, so that here, for instance,
Sir Roger de Thumpington buggers the chambermaid
Behind the rectory, near a garden-wall where the
Cotton-nightgowned maiden tosses on her half-filled bed,
Or where the vampire is at his hideous repast
Below some casement opened on perilous moonlight.
Tee-hee! But your own pictures are not for laughs—the stretched
White bat in your framed negative, the ardent shadows
Fornicating with the upright streaks of light below
The rucked-up skirts of the old railway arch both amuse
Our high-spirited eyes and instruct our figuring.

In Black and White

Where are we now, then? Unable to remain simply
Autumnal any more, what with markets overfull
Of bad red paintings of late afternoon, I locate
My inner weather for you on the map of the year:
Say it is a spell of cold, of chilled nights in the midst
Of a long Indian Summer struck dumb with its own
Fair *longueurs*, dreaming away from what has almost come.
Early autumn looked to be the time of ripening
Truth, and late birds sang of a long moment of shadows
Coming home early to roost in the perches of light.
But the deep, skeptical frost has come and left its first
Hard mark along the surface of the grounds of our hope.
Here is my time, though desire come and go like daylight.

A Time of Year

Remembering my dear dead black cat sometimes returns
Others to my sight—Christine, her kittens Chatto and
Windus (and Fergie), Emmeline and hers, cross Pumpkin,
Bertha of the placid gray, and quiet young Eggplant,
Flora, Bert, nasty Zoltan, Wolfgang and Ludwig's sweet
Mother Priscilla (out of whom by Wilson they were);
Where are the Others' cats I knew—Georgia, Maisie, Wow
(Of these only noble Rose remains). Where are they now?
And where are all their days, the yesteryears and images
That melt like black snow along a dark, familiar rug?
Furred felicities absent them from us in a while;
Months ago I'd promised you something for poor Wolfgang:
What can be said of dead cats that is not dead itself?

What can be said of dead cats? That is not dead itself
Which can escape the icy caress of accurate
Memory (and, you might add, make her stuffy, bemused
Daughters buzz off); come help me then with some fancy-work
(Like all cats I have known he belonged also to you):
A corona for Wolfgang now all of evergreen
Intertwined with catnip which would send him and Ludwig
(His poor gray brother who predeceased him by not quite
A year) literally up the wall. But you must pluck
Faded souvenirs like that figuratively out
Of this wreath lest it wither now like last summer's news.
There can be no catalogue of habits, or times when . . .
No contrived inventory of storied occasions.

No contrived inventory of storied occasions
Could record the string of being holding them in line,
The part of whatever room it was that for a time
Became the place of the cat, lair, veld, branch, hearth or crag.
And yet now—even with your forefinger at my lips—
I reform unutterable losses, reaffirm
What I was making of him alive. Dead now a year,
He is in my hands; I feel him draped around my neck,
Hear the all-but-silent fall of paw on midnight floor,
Drops of some tincture of the Absolute. Absence breeds
Presences in the cells it hollows out in the rock
Of our days, and I can't wonder how, in shudders of
Remembering, my dear dead black cat sometimes returns.

Requiescat

Images of place that loss commanded one to set
Up—the bright beach, the cold hills, the meadow, the pinewoods—
Wait about the available nearby space, open
To any visitors, until nightfall, when, folded
Home, they loll more easily about, no longer prey
To misdevotion, but gentle idles of the page.
And yet now, having got wind of you, the crowds of pines
Stir into assertion; the hills whistle through their rocks;
The beach conjoins its own interpretive roars. And thus
It is they who address themselves, not to images
Of absence such as they had been, but to a presence:
They who have been spoken vainly to and falsely of
In too many chilly idylls now resound in truth.

Remembering Where

P works on his uncommissioned portrait of the world
Shed of figments, his brush giving substance and taking
Cover from the winter scene which cannot warm to it.
A self-portrait of the face of nature has long since
Been worked up on the artless surface of his pallette.
The dry noises of underpainting are nothing to
The loud solitude of a world unable to come
Together with images of itself. The clouded
Meaning of a sky that P had supposed would speak for
The glimmering, blank land that lay below was silent.
And that land, unclothed even in a light shift of snow,
Lay bare in herself: shivering nakedly though, or
Free of the fabric of dream? Unknowing P daubs on.

Plein-air

The language of the howling wind allows an endless
Tale of winter to be told in one long syllable,
Here where this sea of flowing air has become a mere
Glaring of diffuse and mindless light, as unaware
As each dumb, chilling mid-day is of its transience,
Of how it will be grasped by the comprehensive dark.
Everything we see in such light is an optical
Allusion, and not to the winter of sunny noons,
Of smooth-packed snow gleaming in the farmyard, icicles
Eyeing the ground under the barn, of the white shed where
A dairymaid still churns by hand away at the tub
Of metaphor. Not to that, but to the fact-ridden
Land of the unfair cold space, of the unblinking time.

Grounds of Winter

After the midwinter marriages—the bride of snow
Now of one body with the black ground, the ice-heiress
Bedded with her constant rock, the far hills of one mind
With the bare sky now, and the emperor of rivers
Joined with the most recent of his flowing concubines—
After the choirs of the cold have died on the late air,
Low now as our unagitated humdrum heartbeats
Still go about their irreversible chores again,
You and I have heard the song of the long afterword:
The phrases of the moon crooning to the fields below,
The cracking language of frozen forests whose summer
Harps were long since smashed, and the profound, recurrent vow
This bright stream's soft echoing answer rings to the woods.

Metathalamia

Cras amet qui nunquam amavit, quiquam amavit cras
Moriatur—"those who never loved before will love
Tomorrow; those used to loving will tomorrow come
To die"—The old refrains all come down to this: either
Reduced to *tra-la-las*, at whose regular return
Children look at each other and, smiling, mouth the words
And old people nod heads in time, or, if they retain
Meaning at all, they always end up in whispering
"*Death*" in the deep chambers hidden in among their tones.
That is how *Greensleeves*, her smock stained from love in the grass,
Outlasts all the boys who had a go at her. That is
How *nonny-nonny-no* etcetera can survive
The next stanza, and the next, and the next, and the next.

Breaking off the song of the refrain, putting the brakes
On the way that the ever-returning chorus tends
To run away with the whole song—well, that may well be
Breaking away from a frightening joyride before
The wrap-up of metal around some tree or other.
Yes, you say, *but something has to get out of hand so*
That we can go on: and, yes, I answer, but better
Let it be the new material in each stanza
That bridles at sense, reckless of disaster, and leaps
Up into the less and less trustworthy air. The same
Old phrase comes back anyway, waiting for what we say
To be over and done, marking its time, the heavy
Burden of the tune we carry, humming, to the grave.

Refrains

73

Old iambic ways of walking helped us amble past
Look-alikes among the flowers, telling them apart;
Objects contemplated for their singleness remained
Clear of how our thought objects to such naïve beliefs
As in flowers-in-themselves; and powers that subject
Nature so impressively to notice and to long
Memory themselves are subjects of the Empress Mind.
But our fluid, modern stride drowns outlines of nouns and
Verbs in its impatience. Subject of my thoughts, object
Of my desire, knower and the known, run together
On flattened paths. You and I hold hands across our verbs
Of being: who then is subject, who object? Do not
Think I quibble! This is a matter of mind and world.

Our Distress

M's verses (wrote the boring lady bard now dead) smelled
Of the lamp; and aside from how they are still fragrant
With day, with night, with the many subordinating
Twilights, the lady knew little of the ways of lamps:
Tallow on the white bear's fur east of the sun and west
Of the moon; oil from Psyche's trembling hand; the cold blue
Light cupped in the sconces on the walls of hell that showed
The dear, careful brow of Eurydice traversing,
Behind one, the rocky way up and out (let alone
The kind of lamp that burns eight days on one evening's oil);
The metallic smell of my small flashlight sweeping out
Pale demonstrations in the sky of the summer night
That awakened my wide, thirteen-year-old longing eye.

The ways of lamps are dark, their light guarded by shadows:
Would one have had M write by moonlight, then?—that had been
Bottled for bedroom use long before the lady bard
Was born. All of which brings me to this matter of light:
The old study-lamp you brought me long ago, its cocked
Head looking with an inner light at the opened page
Of Alpha's welcoming gaze, or Beta's turning back,
Or Gamma's belly, or Delta's triangle of fur
Where soft portals have been touched by adoring hands of
Shadow, or solemn Epsilon's hand in hand of mine.
As hot as it is bright; sun, moon and constellations
That guide our works and nights, your lamp smells of M's poems, yes,
And all the other nifty redolences of the world.

Lady with the Lamp

75

Your softened shadow now when you come up quietly
Behind me, falls across the place where I am, and most
Particularly cancels the sharper-edged, dark grey
Shadow, dancing irritably, of my writing hand,
Which swallows up the first letters of these very words
Even as I write them out now, so that, in them, "*the—*"
Emerges into light on the left only as "*—m*"
Lies buried in the handy darkness surrounding its
Generation. But that your shade is like light itself
Making clear the story of starting up and ending,
I might have thought that this shading of hurried letters
Was your work, taking back what you knew to have been yours
Of what, here by lamplight, I thought to originate.

Replevin

"*It's a long lane that has no turning*": *Comment upon*
This saying—the written part of an entrance exam
Taken long ago produced I don't remember what
Kind of bluster from me about how a small "indeed,"
After the first word, would help the syntax out a lot.
Construing comes first; then putting wrong constructions on
The hoary old rightnesses had better claim our time.
Very well, then: The very long lane, the longest one,
Has indeed no turning, narrowed so that two cannot
Pass at one time, stretching further out than all desire.
(Longing is short enough: having at last is nothing,
Or even less than nothing—loss. For which, witness the
Brevity of soul, and darkness's longevity.)

The Long Lane

Unanswered, our riddles remain wise and beautiful
In their impossibility of is and is-nots, ones
And manys at once, fluctuating numbers of legs.
The Gordian knot was gorgeous if you stopped to look.
Solving them shoots down the angels of their oddity,
And the prize that thunks down on the hard ground at one's feet
Might as well have been store-bought. One must always recall
The puzzle in the elusive thrumming of its flight,
Or be left with garbage. Like the punned and anagrammed
Crossword, finally finished on that scrap of magazine:
What's it good for now? Eating a ripe peach on? Fold it
Up into a paper airplane, send it flying out
A window of the city, raising questions anew.

Being Puzzled

Unless the green traffic-light were reduced by my crude,
Narrowing regard to a cold eye of permission,
Pursuers would honk like geese in fury, and rightly
So. Unless the red always dutifully remained
A button pushing into my centers of arrest,
There would be crashes and much expensive body-work.
But unless, at least three times a day, that disc of green
Did not demand that its fables be unfolded, that
One wonder what kind of boundless color of ocean
On a fine day poured into a broth of the tinctures
Of grasses and fir—boughs—that its particular green
Lose that dumb tone of command—then what? Then nothing: there
Would be no engine at all worth pampering with gas.

Go Ahead

"Flat Parnassus, super-highway, carrying your freight
Of fact, such as that I am here and that she is there,
That each mile I move toward her may bring me no closer
To the end of longing"—so I sang as the long band
Of road unrolled, fringed with all the emblems of my flight:
Socony's Pegasus flew by in scarlet, Tydol's
Wingèd *A* showed that the letter outflew the spirit,
The golden Shell of pilgrimage openly gave up
The highway's echoed roar to my obedient ears.
My heart was in images of the West—I, buried
In the heart of the East, drawn by film after gray film
To the dust-stung ruins of our far deserts, before
The roads opened up for business and closed down for song.

Highway, 1949

My musings on your past have been filled more than once with
An ancient friend of yours, that lover of horses and
Of a far star, who studied, fought and sang, and yet scrawled
Philippics against his own encroaching self, raising
The citizenry of his soul to bear arms against
Bare arms and pale thighs denied him when his bright star fell
From the sky into a rich marriage with someone else.
He could not refrain from bridling at the groom, but all
That stuff of intricate muttering and blunt quibble
Kept the lost lady's name alight among the hosts of
Inconsiderate stars. With us, quite the opposite—
Your undying name preserves my mortal one: my work
Carves out the room for your memorializing play.

An Old Beau

Maurice Scève found the tomb of Petrarch's Laura, but not
On the sacred ground of the Vaucluse, as the book says:
In the stony figure of his own fictive lady
Of delight, there was the grave of Laura, where she lay.
Asteria Stern—the little girl whose gentle neck
And lovingly twisted braid of hair showing over
The back of the schoolroom chair broke my heart—her clear eyes
Entombed no Delia for Delia had never
Lived; but gazing at her image in my bed, squinting
Through longing's archaic astrolabe, I could learn of
The parallax by which that image was centered in
My field of vision alone: "Stern? Yuck!" (in fact, its then
Equivalent), jeered the silly boys in the schoolyard.

What you have gathered from our talks of Asteria
Stern and the others, then, enables you to propound
Not one more monument, not to build or yet become
Yourself a bit of statuary, but a theory
Of entombment, a walking meditation upon
All memorials, a grammar of storage. So that
When, my hands full of the task-crammed moment, I send you
To the broad, autumnal shelves for something to leave through,
What you come up with always changes in your quiet
Grasp, quickens with all of what it had been meant for it
To become: old star-maps revised in your afternoon
Eyelight; dust blown smilingly from heavy folios,
Joining the stellar whirl of possible golden motes.

Seeing Stars

We say that fact yields truth. But how? mindlessly, as fields
Their crop of grass? hastily, as blackened underbrush
Its rush of blueberries? or reluctantly, as a
Surly guard hands over prisoners to the bearer
Of the great Emperor's seal? But there is this yielding:
In among careless weeds and boring, necessary
Perennials, out of the foul but hopeful magma
Of what indeed it falls to us all to be and do—
Pain, irritation, tedium, rage, sly childishness,
Longing, despair amid the bad weather and the good—
Out of all this muck the particular plant springs forth,
Like a laughing nymph appearing out of the green bank
Of one's own secret river: what the place had been for.

Suppose this were a sprig of myrtle: from what tears, sweat
And wrinkled, ungardened beds does she spring? Dear Olive
And famous but weary Laurel grow here, labelled with
Their names and histories, and were I a husbandman
Of garlands I'd lay out Myrtle whose deepening green
Crowns all our couplings and shades all our passionate beds.
Yet she would end up like all the others: "Look for truth
Not in the dusty books, but in her eyes" Or "Seek not
To penetrate the eastern mysteries, but enter
Her and be truly wise" Or "Myrtle's motion beneath
Your body's hot doings makes the world turn" "Her cry of
Coming will sound for eternity in the long halls
Of desire." Like the others, Myrtle's one for the books.

Grounds and Beliefs

Suppose that you had laid me under an injunction
Never once to utter the syllable of your name;
My soon-to-be-ritualized circumlocution
—*Why, Oh You?*—would always be perforce a questioning,
Not about the nature of your name, but of your will
And the necessities it imposed on my discourse
And, thereby (in the ways I still keep trying over
And over again to explain), on yours. Yet suppose
I called you simply *U*, the twenty-first letter, (*I*
Being the ninth one—both factored by the three of us,
I, you, and the abyss unmarked by any letter).
Even adding this aught to what is, I figure now
To end up with a knowledge of just what I owe you.

Promissory Note

Why do I write you notes in this funny line, long, like
Proletarian fourteeners marching in their way;
Or like the alexandrine, split into groups of three
Beats; or else falling in anapests patterned in fours;
Or else partaking of the noble ten who marched in
Pairs of lines like fighting-men advancing on the words
Of disarray—even the various guerrillas,
Sniping at the phalanxes and squares of orderly
Procession, or moving in jagged—not ragged—lines
Waving bibles like banners, yea, brandishing scripture,
Against old dispensations: like these, unlike them, too,
In that inaudibly marching and dancing loudly
Are both covered by its mandate to be of itself?

Well, the questions of discourse, if drawn out long enough,
Start answering themselves; and yet the point is not
Why you of all people should merit a tone whose own
Clang, whose essential ground, lies both in what it is like
And what unlike—all that is merely personal, as if,
Say, I always kidded you in a Yiddish accent
Sounding as from as close to Wilno as I could feign.
No, the question should be what to make of the way that
Lengths of wordage from the various times of the day—
Questions and answers, puzzle-games, prayers, quarrels and songs—
Of "doubt, desire or emotion," the old standards of love—
Should at night, of themselves, come to stand in quiet lines
Like these, to be recounted, embraced and led to bed.

An Apology for Poetry

149

In the repeating calendar of regret, I turn
A page and find an anniversary: every day,
Every very day comes to another's summoning.
What was happening, then, on, say, 6/6/66?
It was my last summer in this calm town, and before
Leaving, I sat that month and fussed with picture-puzzles
On a quiet back porch—it was one of those warm days
Like 7/7/77, in the first
Summer of returning here, when I sat on a far
Longer porch, numbering some unfallen leaves. Still here,
In this sad town, I sum up such moments now for the
Reckoning day of a month beyond, pervading all
Mere months, where it is always 13/13/13.

Today's Date

150

A day I had forgotten reappeared to me, clad
In a kind of dimmed radiance, neither presenting
Its case, nor yet asking me to represent my own,
But with an equitable air went on its errand
Of merely being there. I called out for you to come
And help me deal with it, but you were somewhere else (out
Looking across the morning water at where the next
Morning would be coming from, it now appears you were).
So that pale day waited, and on being asked in which
Of the volumes of my life it was to be inscribed,
Disappeared with the curious perfume and the most
Melodious twang so common to such vanishings.
That was when you came in with a flaming day-lily.

That's for Oblivion

Where were you back in New York in nineteen forty-two?
The World War won, the Second One then in the winning,
I left one kind of boyhood for its starved antitype.
I still got you mixed up with the genius loci
Of some timely spot, as in nineteen fifty-five when
Rain made Harvard brickwork glisten, my mind drank the light.
Back in New York again in 'sixty-eight, even then
We had met with some kind of recognition, although
I still went my own hasty way too much of the time.
Yet again in Connecticut, my fifty-second
Year is in your hands—and you in mine—who commanded
Candles of ardent occasion to deepen their glow,
Turning nights of passage into moments of lustre.

Lustra

You wrote something on this page last summer. I've just come
Across it. Trying to make sense of it now, trying
To figure out what the errand was you might have sent
Me on—and, even more, what new chore knowing about
What you'd meant then sets up for me now—it's like coping
With the Law that, while being laid down, had been cut up
Into bits with some sort of saw. Thus the commandment
Was to interpret before all else. The puzzling
Injunctions, cross words, prohibitions themselves riddled
With gaps that might or not be loopholes, are more binding
Than bronze statutes standing in public squares, stone tables
Set up in rocky precincts, too easily followed
To have to be obeyed. More binding. More to be sung.

Stories are a matter, though, of radiance, of wholes.
Thus: The day was too clear and bright merely to have been
Exemplary, to blossom and then blast with sundown
And subsequent decay into the mud of the night,
Into one more bit of what could not be *evidence*
That the sun also rises etcetera. The day
Was too clearly that day—when you laughed over spilt milk,
When I cried over spilt wine, when we saw eagles, claw
Hooked in claw, wheeling together over the bald crags—
To be merely that, or to be merely a July
Someteenth. That it was a day like any other meant
That it was totally singular, a story too
Clear, too directly told not to be a parable.

Last Summer

You rely on what I say about you (as do I).
You use me for my purposes I'm ignorant of.
You are given to utter what I must intimate.
You are the Urtext: I have done the illustrations.
You are the ultramarine in which I am enisled.
You are ultimate: I'm intermediate, and so
If you are Ithaca then I must be Ulysses;
I roam indiscriminately toward your urgent shore,
I learn inductively what is understood for you.
I improvise over your recurring undersong.
In and out my mind moves while you have your ups and downs.
I illuminate the darkness that you usher in.
I am a bad liar: you are as good as your word.

You and I

Locked up in this cell as if in punishment for some
Transgression, I pace out daily the determined ground
Between walls of very old stone, knowing no one else
Has ever been kept here. To temper my loneliness
In this room's vast tract of time, I summon up some past
Prisoners, imagine their ancient graffiti here:
"XIII—Atlas holds the sky up, three Hesperides
Stand by in admiration" chiseled on one bare wall
Speaks for a shaping spirit; some figuring one rhymes
"My pent-up thoughts I'll fix, till I have served my time, on
Fibonacci number six which is the seventh prime."
These fancy up the fact of time, while I try to learn
Words of the language in which you'll hand me my parole.

Too Much Freedom

Triskaidekaphobia across the centuries
Kept us seating one more at the table, even when
The extra one was silly or redundant or gross.
Moreover, the new arrangements—the sexes paired off,
The doubled sevens, the mysteries of ten and four—
Masqueraded as reasons, hiding always our fear
Of dangerous and pungent oddments behind the bright
And interesting arrangements that terror had us make.
Like grownups now, allowing the black cats to amble
Across our shadows in the forenoon without alarm,
We can at least, in a poor time for discourse, invite
Exactly whom we please, whom we need: it will be right
In a new shape, finished beyond the old completions.

But then, you say, we go on talking at dinner for
A longer time these days: yes, it too runs over the
Edge of what might have been both decent and effective.
Fine cooking makes one talk of remembered meals; beyond
That there is gossip of the harmless kind, overtures
Toward attractive persons, narratives (the payment of
What one is dining out on) and all the rest of it
That cushions, as in claret velvet, the glittering
Truth that one of us startles the rest by propounding.
We do go on ... but dinner is our serious meal
—Light lunch is not—and even knowing that where we sit
Lingering over drink is at the edge of something
Dreadful soon to happen makes it worth talking about.

In all fairness, when the reasonable noon's blond head
Stretches out along the grass outside our living-room,
In the light of all this, we must remember how once
Loki looked into the place on Valhalla where twelve
Were feasting, added one more, and that was Balder's last
Lunch. On Friday, too. And later on, when there should have
Been only, at the disordered *seder*, the Leader
(Who said: "This is the Bread of Affliction—that's me!—which
Was rushed through its baking on the way out of darkness")
And the Eleven, there was the One more who would help
Make it all twelve again for a while, until they all
Fell one by one, knowing how they had been reclining
On dangerous ground, in the foul shadow of thirteen.

An anniversary cannot be an occasion
Solemn enough any more for breaking out the last
Of the old wine: they have got at yearly intervals
The way they have at public statues, and a private
Moment—a death, a birth, a passage into the next
Chamber that had been awaiting your arrival—has
Been nationalized by the commissars of twelvemonth
So that even the year, to a day, when I first saw
You take form against a background of shadows in that
Room we know so well—even that day has become trash,
Might as well have been proclaimed National Every Day.
Let us drink instead, then, touching glasses, kissing wine
To the memory of tonight last year a month ago.

I heard a rumor that you had dreamed of a New Home
Found by wandering through the mazes of an old one
—A big house in which you were small long summers ago—
Returning to it yearly in dream, and dream of dream,
And then one day in one night's dreaming coming upon
A place where one's bed was, and more: a chamber in which
You handed over your arms, your armor, at the door
Because you did not want them there; a place you never
Hankered after, because when you were away from it
The memory of it dissolved in a solution
Of feeling. That was what bred desire, not for it but
For the someone elses. In your dream you knew this was
The Room of the Thirteen, odd and unaccountable.

But this may yield something: say the room had to be "of"
Some prime, and yet some prime fresh from the barrel, as it
Were, uncomplicated by the ordinary sets
It was the undying cardinal of: *Eleven*,
Even, conjures up The Winning Throw, or strategies
Of passes, high goals, penetrations, backs in motion
—Your room was not about that, though perhaps about what
All that gaming for such long stakes itself was about.
So: the first prime number unattached to meaning, though
Shaded a bit with meaningless fear—at most, fear that
It had no meaning—that was the number of The Room.
Enough, now, lest we both learn that your dream repainted
A number on the door that had been *One*. Or *Zero*.

At thirteen already single-minded Abraham
Smashed up all the idols in his father's house that were
Likenesses of nothing, and turned his inner eye toward
The Lord of Nonrepresentation, whose sole image
Lies encoded somewhere in our own. So at thirteen,
Boys with minds aswim are called up out of their Third World
To sing the old law aloud from an opened scroll, to
Stand up and be counted, and yet more: to count themselves
Fortunate and wise in not coming of age at twelve
Or ten or twenty (months, toes and fingers keeping those
Accounts) but at a time whose number, even more odd,
Signifies its own solitariness and whose square
(One sixty-nine years old?) breeds doubt ("I should live so long!")

Just the right number of letters—half the alphabet;
Or the number of rows on this monument we both
Have to share in the building of. We start out each course
Now, of dressed stone, with something of me, ending where you
Handle the last block and leave something of you within
Or outside it. So we work and move toward a countdown,
Loving what we have done, what we have left to do. A
Long day's working makes us look up where we started from
And slowly to read down to the end, down to a base,
Not out, to some distant border, the terminal bland
Destructions at their ends that lines of time undergo.
Endings as of blocks of text, unlit by the late sun
Really underlie our lives when all is said and done.

Is it the plenitude of seasons, then, the number
Of weeks each one must have for its full hand of cards, that
Gives us a sense of its completeness? The seasons sit
Around the annular table each holding a pure
Run: Winter wields only the spades, Summer brandishes
Hot, black clubs, Spring showers hearts about and Autumn shows
A fall of diamonds in our climate of extremes.
Our parents in Eden, deathless, parentless, were dealt
The perfect year's full hand of intermingled weeks when
Continual spring and fall scattered variations
Of face and number in among the months, whose first names
Were merely decorative. Now seasons play for keeps:
Death deals, and cheats with the false promise of final trumps.

Not for this dull blue, the humdrum stars there to be read
In rows that accrue over the years, but for the quite
Original, true number of stripes which since have bred
Such a changing crew of constellations, was the height
At which the flag flew appropriate and merited.
The oddly-placed hue that tells us to stop is set right
Against tracks of highest clattering overhead.
Windy harp of thirteen strings, a Cretan lyre that might
Descant upon its own fabrications! yet, folded
Away, dreaming of signals from A to Z all night
(Or, as the double-crossed Union Jack would say, "to Zed").
Ensign of life where only interstices are white:
Mud, low sunlight, blood, we begin and end in the red.

Crazy Hans sits on the sidewalk strumming his crazy
Guitar—he has carefully re-fretted the whole thing
And fussed with every string so that touches of sour
Harmony fumble their way into the evening air.
But in his less-than-semi-tones a silent order
Reigns; every unrhyming triad has its reasons
For sounding off as it does: in his thirteen-tone scale
Of falsifications the octaves alone are true.
The blues he sings, confusing in the strings with the hues
And cries of the sidewalk, wraps them all up in a roll
Of night. A chorus totally of blue notes enfolds
The random airs of the corner where he sits strumming.
Crazy Horst across the street roars to his own tom-tom.

At last, the clock has struck thirteen. It would be too late,
Even if that were the matter, to get the clock fixed.
But it rings true and in its way is right twice a day:
Soon after noon it strikes our moment, the time you come
To find me at a table by the window, whereon
Ripening fruit, a thoughtful jug, an uncrumpled cloth
Receiving the shadows can compose a *nature morte*
That is somehow still life, still part of the world of breath.
The clock rings in your arrival, making room in time
For our dear discourse in all its hidden silences,
Room in time among the hurried hours that shoulder
Each other into the cold, dim valley at the end
Of day and night where they shall ever stand shuddering.

That other time of day when the chiming of Thirteen
Marks the hour in truth comes after midnight has made
Its unseen appearance. Then the whole trembling house starts
Gathering itself together in sudden fear, creaks
On the stairs grow tacit, and, even outside, the wind
In the lindens has been hushed. Unlike the time beyond
Noon, when your visitations shape that original
Hour, when we pull the shades down in our space between
Moments totally contiguous in the clocked world,
This black gap between days is no place for us: should you
Creep into my bed then you would find me shuddering
As at the opening of a secret whose shadowed
Power unbroken lay in coupling day unto day.

Thirteen

Let me say first that, although in the demanding light
Of morning the discrepancies rattling our discourse
Speak of a noisier afternoon, what can be heard
Is the sound of things evening up between our two
Conditions—as if we were light and sound disputing
Claims for primacy at the morning of the world; till
The odd, evening hour, neither yours nor mine, but ours,
When our hands reach out to touch like object and image
Moving toward the mirror's surface each through the magic
Space that the other's world must needs transform in order
To comprehend; when our voices have surrounded one
Another, each like some penumbra of resonance.
So that you have the last word now I give it to you.

At the End of the Day

Notes

6: "altogether inconvenient . . . memory", George Eliot, *Daniel Deronda.*

11: "*M'aidez!*" the cry of distress, became "Mayday," the international signal of same.

12: cf. Emerson, "Hamatreya."

21: The hexagram made of the stars of the thirteen original colonies is on The Great Seal of the United States, verso (see a dollar bill, verso).

22: Zechariah 5:1; Ezekiel 3:1.

27: $28,561 = 13^4$

39: George Santayana would tear signatures out of books for his day's reading in the Pincio in Rome, disposing of them after perusal.

44–45: Philemon and Baucis.

47: He looks like Walt Whitman from a distance.

51: A sonnet is buried here.

52: The Thames in Connecticut is pronounced as written, /θeymz/; the Jordan is a stream running through the campus of Indiana University.

56: The parabola is rather like Saarinen's in St. Louis.

68: The names of many letters of the Hebrew alphabet are dispersed throughout.

73: Viola to Feste: "They that dally nicely with words may quickly make them wanton".

78: The sonnets of Meredith's *Modern Love* have 16 lines.

85: Line 7 is (needless to say?) the middle line of the poem.

101: A wise Duke—such as Federigo da Montefeltro.

109–111: After, long after, the twelfth-century providential hymn, *ki hinne cachomer.*

117: "Either because . . . had" is Hazlitt on *Paradise Regained.*

97

131: *"Cras amet qui nunquam amavit quiquam amavit cras amet"* is the formerly famous refrain of the *Pervigilium Veneris* ("Those who never loved before will love tomorrow; those used to loving will tomorrow come to love").

133: Acephalic iambic through line 7.

150: The "curious perfume" and the "most melodious twang" are from John Aubrey's digression from his briefest life, of one Nicholas Towes.

163: The acrostic can be seen at once. The terminal letters' acrostic is for Your eyes only.

166: The rhymes on red and white perhaps need not be pointed out; the blue rhymes do indeed mark out the field in the upper left.

Index of First Lines

JOHN HOLLANDER

John Hollander's first book of poems, A CRACKLING OF THORNS, *was chosen by W. H. Auden as the 1958 volume in the Yale Series of Younger Poets;* MOVIE-GOING AND OTHER POEMS *appeared in 1962,* VISIONS FROM THE RAMBLE *in 1965,* TYPES OF SHAPE *in 1969,* THE NIGHT MIRROR *in 1971,* TALES TOLD OF THE FATHERS *in 1975,* REFLECTIONS ON ESPIONAGE *in 1976,* SPECTRAL EMANATIONS *in 1978, and* BLUE WINE *in 1979. He has written four books of criticism,* THE UNTUNING OF THE SKY, VISION AND RESONANCE, RHYME'S REASON *and* THE FIGURE OF ECHO *and edited both* THE LAUREL BEN JONSON *and, with Harold Bloom,* THE WIND AND THE RAIN, *an anthology of verse for young people, an anthology of contemporary poetry,* POEMS OF OUR MOMENT *and was a co-editor of* THE OXFORD ANTHOLOGY OF ENGLISH LITERATURE. *He is the editor (with Anthony Hecht, with whom he shared the Bollingen Prize in Poetry in 1983) of* JIGGERY-POKERY: A COMPENDIUM OF DOUBLE DACTYLS. *Mr. Hollander attended Columbia and Indiana Universities, was a junior fellow of the Society of Fellows of Harvard University, and taught at Connecticut College and Yale, and was Professor of English at Hunter College and the Graduate Center,* CUNY. *He is currently Professor of English at Yale.*